MDE)

KU-525-217

Please return/renew this item by the last
date shown. Books may also be renewed
by phone or internet.

- www.rbwm.gov.uk/home/leisure-and-culture/libraries
- ☎ 01628 796969 (library hours)
- ☎ 0303 123 0035 (24 hours)

www.rbwm.gov.uk

Royal Borough
of Windsor &
Maidenhead

# CLASS WAR

# CLASS WAR
## A TEACHER'S DIARY

### ANONYMOUS

Biteback Publishing

First published in Great Britain in 2021 by
Biteback Publishing Ltd, London
Copyright © the author 2021

ISBN 978-1-78590-687-9

10 9 8 7 6 5 4 3 2 1

A CIP catalogue record for this book is available from the British Library.

Set in Trade Gothic and Minion Pro

Printed and bound in Great Britain by
CPI Group (UK) Ltd, Croydon CR0 4YY

*To my father*

*A friend of mine read this manuscript and asked me if this was all true. I quoted Picasso: 'We all know that Art is not truth. Art is a lie that makes us realise truth.' 'Look,' said my friend in response, 'Is it true or not? And never mind all yer ol' bollix.'*

# 17 JANUARY

## SONNETS

So far, this unit of work hasn't been working with 9H. It's an old unit. Decent classes have always responded to it. 9H couldn't see it far enough away. I started with 'Anthem for Doomed Youth' and 'Futility', Wilfred Owen, because they've just finished reading *The Boy in the Striped Pyjamas* and I wanted to segue seamlessly into the poetry unit while continuing the war theme.

'Anthem' was disappointing. The class on 'Futility' was an absolute bitch. I'd have got more of a response from the war dead themselves. Jane, the brightest in the class, closed her eyes at one point as if falling asleep. It was first two on a Monday morning but, fuck, that's no excuse – except if it's my excuse. I kept her back at the end and let rip at her and two of her mates. I needed someone to shout at. I paraphrased 'Futility': 'I felt like moving you lot into the sun to see if it would bring you back to life.' That wasn't bad as teacher sarcasm goes. Aside from that it was the usual shit. Bark but no bite.

Now, it was Shakespeare – 'Shall I Compare Thee to a Summer's Day?' Told them it was the most famous sonnet in the language. Is it? Don't know, but I needed an opening. Ten minutes in, they were starting to get it. What was it about this and not about Owen? Was it just a different day, a different mood? What about my mood? Every lesson has its own biosphere, to be measured on a scale of disappointment. But I think 9H liked that it was a love poem; here was someone supposedly writing to someone they loved. I sprinkled this with the conjecture that the loved one might have been a young man, that Shakey might have been a bit of a paedo, which wasn't as frowned on back then. Contemporising, always a good idea: some zeitgeist controversy. (Maybe that was the problem with Owen – so, war is bad. We know that already. What else you got?) Yeah, they liked that. Lapped that up. Even if Shakespeare was a kiddie-fiddler, at least it took him out of a textbook and made him human. They also liked the simplicity of the idea of comparing someone to a summer's day: the poem as a bit of a game. I hesitated to use the word 'conceit' and talk about John Donne and George Herbert and all that crew. Didn't want to balls this up. 'So, summer days can be too warm, too cold, too short; they can have rough winds, be overcast. They're not all they're cracked up to be,' I said.

But what about the rest of it – 'thy eternal summer shall

not fade'? 'Death shall never brag thou wander'st in its shade, when in eternal lines to time thou grow'st'? He's never going to grow old? He's never going to die? What's that all about? Has Shakespeare lost the plot?

I had them. This was one of those moments a teacher must cling to that almost – *almost!* – make up for the rest of the shit. Here was a group of young people, and me and William Shakespeare had got them interested in a piece of literature.

'OK, he's better than a summer's day. I can buy that. But how can he never grow old? How can he never die, people?'

We read the last two lines again: 'So long as men can breathe, or eyes can see / So long lives this, and this gives life to thee.' They looked at those lines, every set of eyes in the class. Some mumbled the lines to themselves. I pointed to 'this' on the board. 'What is "this" – "So long lives *this*, and *this* gives life to thee"?'

It was Emily who put her hand up, God love her. 'The poem!' she said. '"This" is the poem!' 'Go on,' I told her. 'Explain.' And she did. 'So long as people are still reading the poem and thinking about this young man, he will never die. He'll always be alive. His memory. How he was young and beautiful when Shakespeare wrote the poem.'

*The moments teachers must cling to!*

I expanded on Emily's answer, telling 9H that Shakespeare was eulogising Art itself, that great art like Shakespeare's own, or da Vinci's, or Michelangelo's, or Dickens's, or Joyce's will be with us for ever. It will withstand the caprice of the seasons, the march of years, time itself. Political leaders will come and go, empires will rise and fall, but great art will always prevail. I could feel my blood pumping, feel myself getting all misty-eyed. I got up from my seat and swept my arms across the classroom as if across the stretch of centuries, the tide of ages. I could hear stirring music in my head.

Christ, I was good. What am I talking about? I was bloody great! Getting all Robin Williamsy and 'Captain! My captain!' and all that horseshit! Anybody listening in would've thought, this guy certainly knows his iambic pentameters from his glottal stops. Fuck, where are inspectors when you need 'em, the bastards?

Then I had a brainwave. There was half an hour left of a double class. The plan was to give them a comprehension exercise on the poem. But I didn't want to kill the thing. There's that line in the Charles Causley poem: Timothy Winters 'shoots down dead the arithmetic-bird'. Well, this was a Shakespeare bird. They very rarely fly. I didn't want to hack its wings off. I decided to ask 9H to write a poem entitled 'Shall I Compare You to a Winter's Day?' I tried this before, a few years back, with a pretty good class, but it didn't quite come off. At the time, though, I didn't put in the necessary prep. I needed to brainstorm ideas about winter, cover the board, let them pick and choose images, think of how they might turn them into metaphors, similes – skeletal trees, frozen lakes, roaring snow blizzards, leaden skies, the cold white sun. Think of someone they didn't like and eternalise them in verse. It was a good differentiation exercise. The brighter ones would try to write a sonnet, try to put in the same beats as Shakespeare, use the same rhyme scheme, maybe even try to change the tone and mood halfway through as in a real sonnet. The less able would cobble together ten, eight, maybe even six lines. But even that was something. There might be a good image or two in there that I could praise them to the rafters for.

So, 'Shall I Compare You to a Winter's Day?'

I set them to work. Write it out rough in the back of their books. When they were ready, write it out properly in the front, not forgetting to rule their margins, write the title, add the date. Can't forget margins, title, date. When I started out as a student teacher, I told my classes that stuff didn't matter – didn't matter what their work looked like, it was the content that mattered. I used to talk some shite. I still talk a lot of shite, but I know now that presentation is king. To anybody who picks up my books – especially parents – it has to at least look like their offspring are learning something and not like a blind drunk's teaching them. Rule number one: protect yourself at all times.

And there they were, writing away. A class that I hadn't been looking forward to suddenly had taken off. Sometimes happens when you wing it. Other times you spend a lot of time preparing and the thing just falls flat. Life, what?

Five minutes left now. Packing-up time. They would have to finish for homework. But had anybody got anything so far? Anybody want to read anything out?

Jeff's hand went up like it was a Nazi rally. I like Jeff. He keeps a ferret at home. The ferret's called Nathan. Anybody who keeps a ferret named Nathan at home is not a bad lad in my book.

'OK, Jeff, away you go. What've you got? Gimme your soul, baby!'

An expectant hush. I didn't have to tell anybody to belt up. Jeff cleared his throat – 'Shall I compare you to a winter's day … Your ginger hair is so gay.'

It's the hope that kills you.

# 18 JANUARY

Caught a smoker today. Well, not so much caught him, more… well, let me explain.

I was on 'escort duty' after school, which involves going out of the exit doors, down the back steps and accompanying the pupils along the path that leads to the buses. I didn't even make it to the path. Coming down the steps – this about ten metres from the exit door – I noticed a lanky boy, with lots of acne and huge owl glasses, with something small and white wedged in the corner of his mouth. It looked like a filter for a roll-up cigarette. Nah, couldn't be, I said to myself. No one could be so blatant. Then, sure enough, to my astonishment, this boy took a packet of tobacco and Rizla papers out of his blazer pocket and proceeded to make a rollie. As I approached him, and as he saw me approaching him, he continued in this endeavour.

I was thinking only one thing: this is a headcase looking for a fight; exercise extreme caution.

The school, like any school, has its fair share of smokers. At break-time they are seen bolting out the exit doors – it's usually the only time they are animated all day – and racing for the far side of the all-weather pitches. There they will form a huddle, about twenty of them, and slobber over a few butts. For the most part, there's no sanction, unless they are totally flaunting it. If I'm the teacher on duty I'll look in their general direction. They'll see me do so. Then I'll move at zombie pace. I remember an Italian zombie movie where a guy had time to change a tyre before the zombie made it twenty yards. Well, that's my zombie pace, giving them plenty of time to get a last puff and then sidle off. That's not cowardice; it's experience. Life's too short to get worked up about smoking. Or it will be short if you keep doing it, which is punishment in itself. That's what I tell myself, anyhow (hypocrite and twenty-a-day man that I am).

So there's no problem, not unless they're practically blowing smoke in your face and telling you to fuck off.

Now here's yer man.

I looked around for any other teachers. There weren't any. They'd be on duty out the front of the school. I didn't know this guy at all, y'see. Rule number two: know your enemy.

'Excuse me,' I said, nice as pie. 'What do you think you're doing?'

He looked genuinely taken aback. 'Wha?' he says.

'What's your name?'

'Farquhar.'

'And your first name?'

'That's my first name.'

'Your first name's Farquhar?'

'Yeah. What's wrong with that?'

Somewhere in the back of my brain I remembered a Billy Connolly joke about Farquhar and Tarquin and Rupert and the rest of the Oxford Boat Crew. Somebody christened this child Farquhar? I wasn't surprised he wanted to die before his time. *Farquhar!* Why wasn't he lying in a pool of blood? Why hadn't a few bullies kicked the living shit out of a guy called Farquhar, with those big glasses and that acne? But Farquhar had other surprises.

'OK, Farquhar,' I said, beginning again, 'what do you think you're doing?'

'Rolling a cigarette,' he said, as cool as you like.

Ah, fuck, I thought to myself, he's a lunatic. Any moment now I'll be showered in a mountain of furious acne.

I attempted sarcasm. 'You do know you're not allowed to smoke in the school grounds, don't you?'

For the second time, he looked nonplussed. 'Whaddya mean?'

Teachers get used to repeating themselves. It's not a problem. 'You're not allowed to smoke in the school grounds, Farquhar.'

'You're not?'

He was serious. I could tell he was totally serious. The acne on the lines of his forehead reddened as these lines creased together in a display of thought. This boy must have been fourteen or fifteen and he didn't know that it wasn't permitted to light up as soon as you stepped out of the school doors.

'In my old school it was OK.'

'Was it really?' I continued rhetorically, in that annoying, sarcastic, sing-song tone teachers adopt. 'Well, it's not allowed in this school. You're not allowed to smoke on these school grounds.' I pointed to the eight-foot fence at the other end of the all-weather pitch. 'That's where the school grounds end.' I tried a gambit. 'But even then, Farquhar, even outside the school grounds, you're not allowed to smoke, because it's illegal for you to smoke until you are eighteen.'

I awaited his response. That forehead was going again, the acne flame-red. The wait was worth it, because Farquhar finally said, 'That's a bit shit.'

He said this not like the law was an ass, but like this was news to him.

I looked deep into those muddy pools behind his thick glasses. I never call a child stupid. I'll call them plenty of other things, but I avoid that word. I avoid it because, for the most part, I don't believe it to be true. I've taught plenty of children who didn't know a consonant from a hole in the ground, children who were semi-literate. Then I've met them years later and they're running their own businesses and filling in their own tax returns. They weren't stupid; school simply wasn't for them. Education, in the way we hot-house them and make them sit still for hours on end and recite Shakespeare, and try to convince them that Philip Larkin wasn't a dirty old man in a mac but a really important poet: well, they're not buying it. There are a few exceptions, of course. I remember Malcolm. Malcolm's class had to sit an exam to assess their ability relative to age. The pro forma on the front of the paper asked them to fill in their name, sex and date of birth. When I looked at Malcolm's front page he had only filled in his name. I asked him his date of birth. It was something in April. I told him to write it down.

'But which month's that?' he says.

'Sorry?' I says.

'Which month is that?' he repeated. I was silenced for moments. Was this some higher form of questioning I was unfamiliar with? Then I got it. He had to write down the month as a number and didn't know April was the fourth month of the year. That done, he now had to fill in his sex. He looked blankly at me. I didn't want to say 'sex' because that would only send a titter round the class. I smiled. 'Male, female, Malcolm – what's it to be?' Malcolm's pencil hovered but still he didn't fill in the box. But this wasn't some protest at the rigid oppression of sexual signification. Rather, it was incomprehension. 'Male, female...' says Malcolm. 'What's that mean?'

There's no way around it. Forget not knowing April is the fourth month of the year, to get to secondary school and not know what male and female is... *that's stupid!*

Or is it?

Or is it rather a colossal state of neglect? Did nobody ever talk to this child? Did nobody ever read him a bedtime story or sit him down and ask him how he was doing? I'm talking normal human interaction. Love and all that shit. The kind of shit where you get an idea of who you are, and what the world is, and what's in it, and how you might try to negotiate it. Was his home life something I had no conception of?

Back to Farquhar. Jesus, I still couldn't get over that name.

'Didn't you know that, Farquhar?'

'Nobody's ever said anything.'

'What about your parents?'

'Me da buys me fags.'

'Does he now?' I said, and ventured another gambit. 'What about your drink?'

'Aye, that too.'

# 23 JANUARY

Today was a good day.

One of those blessed days.

I had a double with 10P. We were finishing off Robert Swindells's novel about homelessness on the streets of London, *Stone Cold*. The book is award-winning, though Christ knows why! It's filled with ludicrous plot holes and characterisation as thin as Farquhar's fag papers. Yet kids respond to it and that's good enough for me. Rather shit that they'll read than not-shit they won't read. So screw you, Michael Morpurgo and Frank Cottrell-Boyce, give me Robert Swindells and David Walliams any day!

Anyway, we finished *Stone Cold* then watched an equally terrible BBC Two dramatisation of it. In fact, terrible doesn't do it justice; excruciating, more like. Peter Howitt – whom you might remember as Joey Boswell from *Bread* and who also wrote and directed the film *Sliding Doors* with Gwyneth Paltrow – plays a serial-killing ex-army sergeant. It's a performance he will very likely have banished to the furthest recesses of his unconscious if he has any shame. The other actors aren't much better. So why watch it? Kills a few periods, that's why; keeps a difficult class quiet, that's why; while they're watching it, I can prepare other classes or get some marking done, that's why.

Rule number three: when you're getting it easy, take it easy.

Then I had two frees. Lost one of them to cover a lesson, but that was OK. The nightmare with a lost free is that you get a class of head-bangers who haven't been set any work by the absent teacher. Thankfully, this was a bunch of reasonable fifth years who had been set some work. They didn't do much of it but at least their books were open, if not their minds.

After that it was a double with 8D. This class had become a real pain in the ass over the last month or so. Always happens with first-year classes. New to the school, they take about three months to work out the lie of the land and then around Christmas they start to raise their heads. That means January and February are usually spent trying to make them lower them again. I say three months, though I remember one notable class of first years who threw their heads up from day one. They had been in my class fifteen minutes when a blonde-haired girl called Roisin put her hand up and straight out said, 'I want to take a piss!' At least she put her hand up. 'What – right there?' I says, quick as you like. In response, Roisin whinnied like a horse that hadn't seen fresh grass in for ever. Didn't need Nostradamus to predict the shit she and her mates were going to cause.

But, anyway, as I say, 8D were becoming a bit wearisome.

Dislikeable, too. A class very short on manners. I can put up with most things, but a lack of manners makes my teeth grate. I'm a bit like Hannibal Lecter that way. If I lend someone a ruler, I expect a 'thank you'; if someone needs to use the bathroom then an 'excuse me' and a 'please' would be nice. Not so with 8D; they were just rude. Not all of them, but enough of them that I was beginning to be rude back, or sarcastic when I didn't need to be. I had to get a grip, change my approach. Who was it who said that it's the teachers who do the learning and not the pupils?

I greeted them with a smile. I asked Jason at the back how the football game went against the rival school a few days previously; asked Damien why he didn't make the team, that I'd seen him playing on the all-weather pitch at break-time and he looked decent. Louis was on time for a change and I complimented him on that (though it was hard not to be sarcastic). All standard stuff, trying to create an atmosphere that suggested we were all human beings together, that it wasn't me against them. And today it worked. I wanted them to look at two poems in preparation for the assessment the following week. One of them was 'First Day at School' by Roger McGough. I'd removed the title from the photocopy I gave out and I asked them to consider where the poem was set. They identified 'the bell', 'playground' and 'uniform' in the first stanza. So we were in a school. I asked them to think about whose voice they might be listening to as we read the rest of the poem.

It was Robert who got it.

First, let me tell you about Robert. He's sitting at the base

end of a Level 2. To the layman, that's around Primary 3, i.e.
Robert has the communication skills of a seven-year-old,
and a limited seven-year-old at that. He is able to read only
the most basic sentence; his writing is an indecipherable
mix of whorls and jagged lines: imagine yourself drunk and
trying to write a paragraph in complete darkness, and that's
Robert's scrawl. Besides this, I have yet to hear him laugh.
He's smiled the odd time but mostly he looks like he's going
to cry. Not once since the start of the year has he come into
class with all of his books; he's either forgotten his novel or
his homework textbook or his exercise book. This isn't deliberate. The child has no organisational skills. So mostly
he sits mute. On a few occasions, I've asked him to read
a sentence from the class novel, Roald Dahl's *Boy*. At this
invitation, his entire body would spasm, he would seem to
lose control of his arms and they would flutter by his sides
like he suddenly wanted to dance. That's how scared he is.
Again, think of yourself, day after day, being forced to do
something you are really terrible at and that you hate.

OK, forget that, that's your life, right?

But anyway: today, Robert was sensational, for whatever
reason. Discussing the first poem, an exercise in simile and
metaphor called 'Fireworks' (I didn't know the author: I
should have but I didn't), he was his usual self. Not a word, not
a flicker. He was looking at the board but it might as well have
been a window. Then we moved on to the McGough poem.

'So who might be speaking in the poem?'

Robert's hand went up. Slowly, tentatively, like a drowned

man's arm lazily floating to the surface, gradually emerging from some aqueous depth… but it went up.

'Yes, Robert?' I asked, hoping I'd kept the surprise out of my voice, though I probably hadn't.

'It's somebody's first day.'

'First day where?'

'At school.'

'How do you know that?'

'It says all the children are bigger.' His arms were beginning to jerk.

'Maybe it's just a small child. How do you know it's the first day?'

He gulped like he was coming up for air – like he hadn't drowned, like he was just a bad swimmer. 'She doesn't know what a teacher is. She thinks a teacher makes tea.'

'Brilliant,' I said. 'Anything else tell you that?'

'She doesn't know what a lesson is. So she hasn't been in one yet.'

'Brilliant,' I repeated.

His arms dropped and he put his head down as if this had all been too exhausting.

Why had he responded to the poem? I don't know. Maybe the fear the child felt in the poem was akin to the fear Robert felt every day. Maybe this place was as alien to him as it was to the child? Maybe he remembered his own first day at school, something seared indelibly in his memory like a trauma.

But I come back to a point I made in an earlier entry

– Robert is not stupid. Rather, his mind is not functioning as it is supposed to function. Answers on a postcard as to why.

I am a cynical bastard. I curse my profession daily. There are many, many days when I can't see my job far enough away, many mornings when those periods stretch out in front of me like a long, dark tunnel where the light is an approaching train. Yet I recognise my responsibility. I have to try to do what I can for these kids, some of whom are very damaged. Doubtless a lot of the frustration that teachers feel, good teachers – and I would be loath to count myself amongst their number – is that they can't do nearly enough; that the damage is irreparable.

After lunch, it was 9H and 'Shall I Compare You to a Winter's Day'. Jennifer wrote this:

Shall I compare you to a winter's day?
White frozen ground, under the dead sun.
Bare trees, washed out sky,
Treading on the silver lake –
All these, nothing to the ice in your heart.
Landscape drained of colour,
Blankets of leaden clouds,
Dull brown and greens as far as the eye can see.
Words twisted like branches,
Between your frost-bit smile.
But spring will come
The world will thaw
There will be new flowers
And I will walk in the light.

It's got fourteen lines, like a proper sonnet, and that change of tone toward the end. It's not a work of art but it is a first draft and it has something of what art is supposed to be – a ring of truth about it, an essence of conviction and, most importantly, a beating heart. When Jennifer finished reading it out to the class, there was silence for seconds until Peter said, 'Wow, that's dope, sister!'

Couldn't have put it better myself.

What did I say about hope?

# 29 JANUARY

The Head came in today to do her inspection. She's new, and an ex-inspector, and she wanted to spend a period in everybody's room. She said she just wanted to sit in on an ordinary period, no bells and whistles.

Lucky, that, because she wasn't getting any.

I don't trust inspectors. This isn't any inbuilt, irrational, knee-jerk prejudice. I was first inspected two years out of college. The inspectors were coming in Monday, Tuesday and Wednesday, writing their report on the Thursday and delivering their verdict on the Friday. Even as I write this, that word 'verdict' sticks in my craw. Who are they to judge a school when they've never taught in it? That may seem simplistic, but it gels with my experience of them. Anyway, they were coming, and seasoned teachers were shitting themselves. The card table at lunchtime was packed away and dirty pictures taken down. (I'm joking about the latter, but the guy who worked next door to me did take down the 'Arbeit Macht Frei' banner he had stapled above his white-board.) So Monday morning arrived and, wouldn't you know it, an inspector landed at my door first two. The class were a challenging one: very much lower ability. Pearse was in it. The week before he had had to be restrained by the Vice-Principal after a bout of chair throwing, and was forcibly removed from my room while shouting, 'Put me down, ya gay cunt, or me da'll fuckin kill ya!' Pearse was about three foot three and, boy, did he have wee man syndrome. So there he was, along with a few other smiling assassins who didn't give one sweet damn that my teaching career was on the line.

And... the class went like a dream. I had them organised into groups, each group differentiated according to ability. This was bells and whistles with bells and whistles on. It was like spinning plates, moving from one group to the other, cajoling them and warning them in equal measure, utterly exhausting for an hour and ten minutes, but, finally, at long last, at long fucking last, the bell went.

The class departed and I was left with the inspector. She looked like an inspector; like the last time she laughed was when Bambi's mother died. 'So,' she says, letting that 'So' linger, 'how do you think that went?'

I'd got my breath back. 'Good,' I said. 'Yeah, it was a good lesson.'

'Really?' she said. 'I didn't see much learning going on.' Those were her exact words. I'll never forget them. And with those words, she exited stage left.

I was flabbergasted. I was utterly floored. Panic gripped me like a hand round my throat. I had another class coming in, but I told the teacher next door – he of 'Arbeit Macht Frei' – to keep an eye on them for a minute. I went straight to the Headmaster and explained what had happened; that I had just taught a really good lesson only to be told it was a piece of shit. He said to leave it with him.

He came back to me at the end of what had been a very long day. I didn't get another visit, but my nerves were shot, confidence gone. If an inspector had walked in, I would have made a genuine balls of it this time. But the Headmaster told me not to worry. 'Not to worry?' says I. 'She's going to hang me out to dry!' The Headmaster shook his head. 'Miss _____ followed that class for the rest of the day. She realises now what a challenge they were. On reflection, she's upgraded your lesson.'

For a minute or so I was too relieved to think straight. The Headmaster gave me a hearty clap on the back and a 'Well done' and left.

Then I could think straight. And I was fit to be carried out of the room like Pearse the week before, only I'd have called that woman a lot worse than Pearse called the VP. What if she hadn't followed that class for the rest of the day? What then? Huh? And why the hell hadn't she come and apologised to me face-to-face for making such a rash judgement, and for speaking to me like I was the shit on her poisoned stiletto?

*Inspectors!*

During a much less dramatic inspection in a different but equally difficult school, I got a chance to sit down and have a coffee with a guy who had inspected one of my lessons. He was friendly enough, mid-fifties, didn't look like the sort to have pictures of Hitler in his bedroom. He talked about his own teaching career – what there was of it. He had taught for a few years in a co-ed grammar school in Belfast. Now, I'm sure even a grammar school's no picnic, but it's a different ballgame. I was in a school with 40 per cent free school meals, with close to the same percentage on the Special Educational Needs register. A co-ed grammar school! What, where little girls pissed themselves at the threat of a black mark for forgetting to back a book?

Again, what right had he to judge my work? Sure, he might have inspected similar schools. Then again, every school is different. I find it interesting – no, I find it infuriating! – that inspectors expect teachers to personalise their approaches to suit the needs of children in their classes, but the ETI (Education Training Inspectorate) have the same inspection process for all schools, regardless of the individual make-up, circumstances and requirements of those schools. No, let them come in and teach my classes for a week – a day, even – then I might pay a little more attention.

As it is, fuck 'em!

There's an article in *The Guardian* today. (Yes, I am that kind of teacher. I do read *The Guardian*, and I've at one time worn corduroy trousers, and jackets with leather patches on the elbows.) The report states that in England, 'recruitment targets have been missed for six years in a row … A third of new teachers give it up within five years … Last year, 10 per cent of all secondary school teachers left teaching.' It goes on to state: 'Inspectors, in future, will take a broader-brush approach, less focused on the minutiae of individual pupils' measurable achievements and more on the big picture.' I know what they can do with their broad brush.

Big picture?

Let me tell you the big picture. To my mind, and I know I'm biased, teaching is the hardest job you can do. But don't just take my word for it. The National Foundation for Educational Research found that teachers endure greater job-related stress than other professionals. A 2019 NFER report concluded that one in five felt tense about the job most or all of the time compared with 13 per cent of those in similar professions. So it's the hardest of jobs. Personally, I'd put nursing up there too. Sure, there's the casualty department on a Saturday night with drunks brandishing knives and bottles, but teachers are daily confronted with a fair share of the recalcitrant and the nasty and the unhinged and the violent. *And we've to teach them!* We've to entertain them, we've to humour them. Every day. Day after day. So quit and do something else, you moaning bastard, says you. Unfortunately, unlike, say, a David 'Just call me Dickhead' Cameron, who can plunge his country into an ocean of steaming shit and then quit and go write his memoirs in the garden shed he bought for twenty-five grand, I haven't that luxury.

On a lighter note, back to my Principal, who was coming in to have a 'little look' at how I do things. As you can guess by now, I didn't have many butterflies in my stomach, acid bile having killed most of them. Smiling conscientiously, I greeted her at the door and then escorted her to a seat at the back, beside the 'glory hole' in my wall. That's right, a glory hole. For those innocents unfamiliar with the term, it comes from pornography, where a phallus would emerge from said hole to be fellated (or so I'm told). In case there was any dispute as to what it was, 'GLORY HOLE' was written neatly around it in an almost perfect circle in black felt-tip pen. The writing was very faded but just about legible. At least the spelling was correct, right? That hole had been in my wall since before this was my classroom. How had it come to be there? What the hell had the teacher been doing? It was probably an accretion. One day, somebody starts digging in the wall with a pen. Another day, somebody else follows up. Soon there's a hole. Maybe the idea is to dig a tunnel and make a bid for freedom. Hey, maybe it was the teacher who started it?

I had asked time out of number for that hole to be plastered over, for going on five years now, and it was still there. And there sat the Principal beside it. God forbid that some horny sod in the next classroom along should pick this inopportune moment to shove his upright member through it. Something wet and fleshy tickles the Principal's ear; she looks around astonished, her mouth yawning open... As I say, God forbid!

After the glory hole, I pointed out the lack of curtains or blinds on the windows. This meant that I was blinded on winter mornings with the low sun and on summer days by the glare. It meant that I couldn't project anything on to the whiteboard because the pupils couldn't see it. Note I say 'whiteboard' rather than 'interactive whiteboard'... *gedout-tahere!* I didn't even have a DVD player. I did have a video player; however, this was part of an ensemble TV unit – y'know, those huge thick Dansette sets that were new about the time Jacob Rees-Mogg was breastfeeding on his nanny's tits (or maybe that wasn't so long ago). Re: the above, it had a 'big picture' and it also had a red sticker on the side to say that it had failed the last electrical inspection. But what the hell, what's a little electric shock against the furtherance of knowledge and the pursuit of truth? Beside all this, the room was a green-yellow colour, a colour like no other – think of a zit grown to such horrendous proportions that it's now turning gangrenous – and had last been painted back in the age when classrooms used to be painted (the '70s?). Seriously, remove the desks and chairs (as someone had done with the blinds and curtains) and splash some blood on the walls and you were in Abu Ghraib.

As for the lesson, it was OK. Mr Chips and Miss Jean Brodie could rest easy. I was giving back books. I'd photocopied a couple of the pupils' pieces of work. Not the best or the worst, but a few in between to illustrate what people were doing right and what a lot of them were doing wrong. It's something I always do. The pupils were responsive; nobody called me names.

The Principal said she was giving follow-up notes after each of her visits – when would I be free to chat? Later in the day?

I told her I'd lost my free later in the day. She said she'd catch me some time. We were all smiles and great buddies. Oh, yes, and she'd speak to the caretaker about the blinds and curtains, and maybe a lick of paint, and the... what was it again?

'Glory hole.'

# 30 JANUARY

Double with 10P and their assessment on the novel *Stone Cold*. In fact, it was a triple. I lost the follow-up free to 10P as well. That's us together for two hours. They looked as pissed about this as me. Happy days and hats off to whoever's doing the timetable. Gimme more, more, more! If this is torture, chain me to the wall, baby!

Plus, *Stone Cold*. As I said, I'm not a fan. Yet I will admit it does allow for some good follow-up exercises. The killer in the book gives us his thoughts in a series of chapters called 'Daily Routine Orders'. In some of these chapters he details how he traps and kills his victims. With 10P I re-read two of these short chapters. In the first, 'Daily Routine Orders 5', the killer describes how he tricks a young homeless man by posing as the manager of a youth hostel. He says the place is full up that particular night, but he might be able to get the homeless guy a bed the following night. In the meantime, he can offer him a kip back in his flat, if that'll help. In 'Daily Routine Orders 7', the killer poses as a security guard when he finds a homeless woman sneaking out the back doors of a hotel having just used the bathroom. He accuses her of being a thief and threatens her with the police unless she comes back to his flat and helps relieve him of a few fluid ounces of sperm. That isn't exactly the language used, but you get the picture. And now 10P had to write 'Daily Routine Orders 8' for their monthly assessment, where the serial killer tells how he traps his next victim, or 'recruit', as he calls them.

Verbatim, Angela wrote this:

Daily Routine Orders 8

It was a biter cold night, most places were closed and not many people were out around the streets. I knew it would be easy to recruit another victim of mine. It had been awhile sinse I had killed my last victim because I didn't want anyone to realise there was 'missing' people who're actually dead because I had killed them, I couldn't make a pattern that would get the coppers onto me.

I live at primrose Hill, nothing much happens here it's more a family/ friendly place to live at know one would think a man like me would live here. I got the closest tube to oxford circus then I got off there and I just strolled about looking for the right person to recruit.

I walked into a 24 hour café and there was a youge girl around the age of 17 soaking with the rain, she was crying buckets of tears and I thought this was just the right person to recruit. The girl was pretty short, hair was greesy looked like it had never been washed before the dirt on her skin was absoutly disgusting. I approached the girl and asked her if she had any place to go to get all washed up but she didn't answer and she seemed like a real bitch so I repeated myself and she looked me up and down and then said she has no where to go. I had to make up a believeable story all sorted, I said to the girl 'awk that's awful, ive my own daughter around your age and wouldn't want to see her in the way you are.' She shook her head and shivered and sobbed I told the girl 'you can get the tube home and stay the night my daughter will help you get washed up and give you a few new outfits and I'll get you food when we get home'. She didn't even think twice and just shouted yes. After that we got on the tube and made our way back to my place.

We walked into my house and it was clean, warm and tidy. I told her to hop into the shower and get washed so that's what she did. She walked into the living room in a white robe and asked where my daughter was and i said she will be home soon then she sat down so I walked into the kitchen and got my homemade tomado soop and spict it to make her sleepy. As soon as I handed her it she ate it like there was no tomorrow. She fell asleep on the couch and I walked up to her and stabbed her to death and then took a picture of the body. I dressed her up a lay her next to the other bodys.

What do you think?

Look at the mistakes. Look at the spelling errors – 'sinse', 'soop', youge', 'know' instead of 'no'. Look at the number of full stops and capital letters that are missing; the words omitted all over the place; the basic vocabulary demonstrated by the repetition of 'walked' and 'got'. This is the 'lowest-ability' group in Year 10, and Angela herself is classified SEN (Special Educational Needs) because of her literacy, or lack of it. She has access to a classroom assistant for a few periods a week. This should be full-time, but such is the budget. The CA has done great work with her, though. Angela *is* making progress. This is the first year she has been prepared to read out loud in class, for instance. She has also made friends; good friends, who will shush everyone when Angela reads and ensure that she is heard in silence and with respect. All in all, she is becoming more confident, even if she still blushes if I so much as look at her, never mind ask her a question.

Boy, is she going to be blushing in my next class with 10P. Because I think this is fantastic.

Look at the spelling from the other end of the telescope. 'People', 'realise', 'actually', 'friendly', 'disgusting', 'approached', 'daughter', 'picture'; she spelt all those words right. Those are all commonly misspelt words. The full stops and the capital letters – there's work to do there. Then again, in this age of phones, this is a problem with most kids nowadays – they don't see the need. But I bet if I sit Angela down and tell her that she just has to concentrate on basic punctuation and go back over the text with a red pen, she'd see most of those mistakes. Words missing, the same. As for the vocabulary, I think we might work on that as a class. Take that last paragraph and explore and tease out how we can improve it – the language, the sentence structure, the word choice. I think there's two periods' worth of work there. Good work, that the whole class would get something out of. Maybe a week's worth, or two. Other stuff I was to move on to will just have to wait.

And that's the problem with the curriculum and target-setting. Rushing through units of work so you can tick a box. It's the problem with lesson plans and all that... shit. (I remember an older colleague of mine who was asked by an inspector – yes, them again! – where his lesson plan was, to which my colleague replied: 'If I still need a lesson plan after twenty years of teaching, I'm not much of a teacher, am I?') If you spot something worthwhile, something that's not part of the plan, then throw the plan out the window; go where your nose leads you. Slow it down, stop altogether. Improvise. Take a chance. As in life.

But back to Angela, because the above is not why I think her work is fantastic. That's not what's made my whole day feel worthwhile and why I would even go so far as to say that I forgive that lost free (and believe me, that's going far: for me, that's the outer limits).

No... *It's Angela's story intelligence!*

Read her piece again. That line about not creating a pattern 'that would get the coppers onto me'. (I love that she calls them coppers.) Then she mentions where she lives, the kind of place where no one 'would think a man like me would live here'. She's getting into this story, she's thinking it through, she's empathising; she's making it real. Then she picks up the girl with the 'greasy' hair. The rest of the class had merely done a re-hash of the other 'Daily Routine

Orders' chapter and pretended that they were a nice guy who ran a hostel that was full for the night. Angela dramatises another scenario altogether, which I would argue is much more plausible than those Swindells actually uses in the novel. The daughter angle is brilliant: 'awk that's awful, ive my own daughter around your age and wouldn't want to see her in the way you are.' Brilliant, I say. It's the perfect way to entice this young girl back to the killer's flat, if the killer is a father and his daughter is back at the flat, and this girl desperately needs a bed for the night… Then that last bit where the killer takes a picture of the body. Where did she get that from? The tomato soup, the shower, the warm clothes, laying the dead body with the others: those are in the novel, but taking a photograph isn't.

She's in his head, I tell you! She's immersed herself so deep in her story that she's had a little glimpse of his madness.

I repeat, story intelligence. Angela has buckets of it. And where's there's story intelligence, there's lots of other intelligence.

It's life, Jim, but not as we know it!

Or as the school league tables would know it. Will Angela gain a respectable C in her GCSE in two years' time and push our percentage up? Will she ever make up for all these present deficiencies in her grammar? I don't know. But whether she does or not, I *do* know, and her other teachers know, and her parents know that this school is working for her in terms of her confidence and her happiness.

'Tis a pity that's not measurable.

# 4 FEBRUARY

February is always the most difficult month in school. Always. That's even with half term in the middle of it. Why? I'm not sure. I just know if there's any kicking-off to be done, it's usually done now. To continue the kicking-off analogy, maybe the school year is like a football season. By this time of year, most fans know how the season is going to turn out and the vast majority are disappointed. Maybe it's the same with the kids. There they were with the hope of early season, looking at the timetable/fixture-list and thinking, 'Maybe with a bit of luck, if I put my head down, this year could be different...' Then there's the grim reality of autumn, when limitations are laid cruelly bare. By Christmas, there's maybe a decent cup-run to cling to. But by winter's end, it's all over and there's nothing left to play for; nothing left to do but... well, call the dinner lady a cunt, which is what someone got suspended for today. This following two other suspensions for a fight. Yesterday, somebody flooded the toilets. There are four suspects, so I've heard. Corey's one of the suspects. My money's on him.

I taught him last year. The first thing I remember him saying to me was, 'Do you wear a wig?' He has this mop of untamed curly hair. I hit back with, 'No, but I bet you wish you did.' That gave the class a titter. That was one-nil to me. If I'd have taken offence it would've been one-nil to him. A few weeks later, I moved him to the front of the class so he was right under my nose. At the back, where he was sitting, he wouldn't shut up. While he was at the front, right beside my desk, he snipped the cable on my phone charger. The phone was already charged so I didn't know anything about it until another pupil came to me in the next period and grassed him up. The grass didn't like Corey. Then again, nobody seemed to like Corey. Still, I wanted to build a water-tight case and cornered a few pupils individually at lunchtime. It was Corey all right. After lunch, I pulled him out of class and confronted him with his perfidy, i.e. the two ends of my phone charger. I expected a denial. I fully expected a denial. Instead, he had this smirk. 'Sweet,' he says. Just like he expected me to, I completely lost my rag and started roaring at him. *Sweet!*

One-all.

But I have to say, as time went on, Corey really trounced me. It was a hammering. Man against boy, except Corey was the man. Much of it was to do with the class itself, though. It was a difficult class. Not discipline-wise – although they weren't the easiest in that sense, either – but more in terms of their needs. There were eight pupils in a class of twenty on a statement, meaning they were somewhere on the Special Educational Needs register, and each needed an Individual

Education Plan. Curiously – unbelievably – Corey wasn't on a statement for his behaviour. In fact, when we were briefed on the new cohort of first years, Corey's primary school Principal had commented on his report card that he was 'fantastic'. Hmm. Despite the fact that Principals are not noted for their sense of humour, I can imagine this one writing that word and then smiling wickedly before dissolving into mad-scientist hysterics of laughter while thunder rumbles overhead. Considering there are approximately half a million words in the English language and about a quarter of these are adjectives, I reckon I could have come up with at least two or three thousand better words to describe Corey, a lot of them some variation on what someone had got suspended for calling the dinner lady.

Anyhow, first of all, the eight pupils on a statement. Generally this meant that each class teacher had to lavish as much praise and encouragement as possible on these pupils, identify key words in the lesson for their benefit, break tasks down into steps using 'Now, Then, Next' strategies, always give short and clear instructions, have each of these pupils repeat the instructions, incorporate peer association into as many tasks as possible, use writing frames, allow time for correcting and redrafting, develop a reward system, leave time for homework to be recorded in a planner and check that said homework had been recorded correctly, and make sure that the planner was on the desk at the beginning of the lesson along with exercise book, reader and any specialist equipment such as iPads (and that these were charged).

Jesus, I'm exhausted just writing this. But OK, I could do all of it. It's a lot of organisation at the beginning and the end of a lesson and also means extra preparation, but that mightn't do me or any of the other pupils in the class any harm. But just let me say that eight SEN pupils in the same class is getting it pretty tight. ('Eight!' I hear a Monty Python-esque voice shout. 'Only eight! You don't know you're living, mate! You don't know you're born!') When I left teacher training, I qualified as a teacher of English language and literature (or *lit-er-a-chore!* as Michael Caine says it in *Educating Rita* when he's seriously pissed), meaning that I was trained to teach pupils who were leaving primary school with a certain level of literacy and carry them on from there, introducing them to the teeming world of ideas and beauty that is the English canon. But no matter if they didn't give a shit about all that 'come hither' malarkey or 'wandering lonely as a cloud' or 'truths universally acknowledged'... I wasn't trained for this. Sure, there's been the odd training day over the years, but nothing approaching what is needed. Eight SEN pupils in a class; it's the equivalent of throwing a punch-drunk no-hoper into the ring with the heavyweight champion of the world. Sure, Sylvester Stallone did it in *Rocky*, but it's easy to lose sight of the fact that despite the upbeat ending and swelling music of that laughable paean to the good old American Dream, Sly actually lost the boxing match and got the shit beaten out of him in the process. So, no, I wasn't trained for this. To illustrate, there were two particular pupils on the statements. According to the info from primary school, one had a 'development delay', meaning he was taking longer to reach certain developmental milestones than other children his age. OK, I thought, so some take a little longer than others: some of my mates didn't buy their first round until they were well into their twenties. However, in the case of this child, it meant he was effectively mute. The other pupil was diagnosed as having SpLD, or 'specific learning difficulties'. Now that's a catch-all term. In this case, specific meant everything. This boy was totally illiterate. He could not perform the most basic of tasks. For instance, he could not write. By could not write, I mean just that – *he could not write!* Yes, he tried, but if I wrote a few words in his exercise book and told him to copy out the letters (that's the level we're talking here), I would return five minutes later to find a different set of letters underneath the ones I had written, as if he was working on a code: a code that involved some letters of the English alphabet and some others that he just seemed to have invented for the hell of it. Put simply, I hadn't a clue what to do with either of these children. Not the first baldy notion. In my view, both of them should have been in a special unit with specialist teachers, educational psychologists, speech therapists and whoever else might come in useful. As it was, they had me. Just me, no classroom assistants. I'll go back to my teacher training: I know how to critique *Wuthering Heights*, say, or 'Dulce et Decorum Est', but I don't know how to teach someone to read as if I was sitting down with a four-year-old. OK, you would take the same approach as a parent with their child when they brought home their first reading book. OK. But remember, these two children I'm speaking of had already been through seven years of primary and that hadn't worked. Hence my question to anyone who would listen (which was no one): what the hell was I supposed to do with them?

So, there I was with these two pupils and the other six children who were on a statement – two of whom were autistic – and eleven other pupils who deserved an education, one of whom was Romanian and had no English whatsoever... and I had Corey.

I remember one Friday I had them for the two periods before lunch. The lesson should have been a good one. I had photocopied the description of Mrs Pratchett in Roald Dahl's *Boy*. It's a brilliant description, teeming with adjectives and adverbs. But crafty bastard that I am, I had tippexed out the adjectives and adverbs and turned the description into a cloze procedure. The class were split into groups and were to discuss and fill in the blanks with their own adjectives and adverbs and justify them: this before the big reveal of the actual text and what it might illustrate in terms of vocabulary. All well and good. Except halfway through, I was seriously at the point of just grabbing my coat, walking out and going home to watch daytime TV. It seemed a better use of my time than this. I was shuttling between the eight pupils on statements, doing my best with them, though my best was beginning to feel woefully inadequate. The developmentally delayed boy... well, he was just looking at me.

I was talking and talking to him but – nothing. With the SpLD boy, I was struggling to decipher code that would have driven Alan Turing batshit. This while hands were shooting up all over the place as other pupils needed help, or one of the statemented pupils wanted me to explain again what I had already explained maybe three or four times (and had them repeat back to me each time). Dealing with this was like trying to close a bulging suitcase. But instead of closing it, the zip was about to break. The zip being me.

Often you feel a class getting away from you. A feeling of mild (or not so mild) panic seizes you. Either you've set the bar too high or too low. But it's too late to change anything so you just push on through to the end and chalk it up to experience. That wasn't the problem here, though. I felt the bar had been set just right. That was a major part of the problem. The requisite challenge was there for everyone in the class but in that perfect calibration I was overwhelmed by the demands being made of me. I couldn't keep spinning all these plates. Not being able to split myself in two – or three, or four – the natives were becoming restless. Chief amongst these natives, of course, was Corey. He had taken to wandering around the class and, as was his wont, annoying people. I let out a roar: 'Get back in your seat!' But this was grist to Corey's mill and he totally ignored me, leaning over someone's desk with his back to me. I think he may even have wiggled his ass.

I could have hit him.

I could have driven my boot up his hole!

For a few delirious seconds, I imagined the deep pleasure it would give me; a pleasure so intense it might even make up for my sacking and subsequent criminal prosecution. With the incessant demands of the other pupils in that pressure-cooker atmosphere, I was about to blow.

I didn't. Instead, I removed Corey from the classroom and sent him to the Year Head. It's something I'm normally loath to do, shunt my troubles off on someone else, but I didn't see an alternative. I was dangerously stressed. Then, without returning to the classroom – they could have been killing one another in there for all I cared – I went to the SENCO, the teacher in charge of Special Educational Needs, and demanded a classroom assistant. If I didn't get one, I was going on the sick.

A week later I got one and she was left in charge of the DD and SpLD boys. At least with those two in harness, I could divide my time just a little bit better.

Re. Corey. By the end of the year, he had stopped even pretending to work. If I asked him to do anything he would look at me, tilt his head, scratch his chin as if thinking about it, then go, 'Nah, couldn't be arsed!' And this was the same in all his classes, with all his teachers. He was suspended I don't know how many times. Didn't give a damn, couldn't have cared less. With a lot of the kids who are causing no end of shit, you can still talk to them. You can pull them aside and ask them what's going on, what the problem is; when they don't have an audience – when they don't have to act the big man or woman – you can sometimes have a half-human conversation. Almost always, they'll drop a little of the bravado. With Corey, even in a one-on-one he was surly, rude and aggressive. As a colleague who also taught him told me, if he could have one wish, he'd ask for five minutes in his storeroom with Corey and a set of knuckle-dusters, 'and fuck the lottery'.

With his fellow pupils, it was the same. I never witnessed one interaction involving Corey where he wasn't trying to annoy someone, make fun of them, bully them. If he was standing in a line, he would drive his knee into the back of the leg of the person standing in front of him. Sitting behind someone, he would be kicking their chair. Every waking moment he seemed to be on the lookout for an opportunity to hurt, humiliate, harass.

What do you do with someone like that? Sterilise them so they can never have children of their own? I'm a leftie; I'm a socialist. I believe that poverty damages people in their soul. I believe that those with money and power have skewed the system in their favour and this involves quite deliberately limiting the life chances of those from a lower social class. Yet I look at Corey and I realise there's a fascist in me too. I don't know much about his family background, except that he had two older sisters, past pupils of the school, who I'm told were lovely children. I've never met his father or mother. But even if there's been recent trouble at home, even if there isn't much money... can it fully explain Corey? Is this just, for want of a better word... *badness*? Nothing to do with environment, nothing to do with socioeconomics?

Just plain badness?

Then I remember Patrick.

I taught him the first year I left college, my first teaching job. I didn't know it when I applied, but the guy I was replacing had just taken early retirement. As a colleague later told me, 'his head was done in'. The Principal gave me some advice when I first went to him about the trouble I was having. 'You'll either sink or swim,' he said. Thanks for that, I didn't say.

It was a nightmare! My timetable involved teaching the lowest-ability class in every year. There was no let-up. One lot of head-bangers trooped out and another lot trooped in. But there was one class in particular: 2D.

They would spit on one another. God's truth. I would be standing in front of them – I say standing in front of them, rather than teaching them, because there was no teaching going on; I was simply the person standing at the front of the room – and anyone might have thought I had just wandered in from the street and was waiting for the rain to go over or something, except I had a suit and tie on and a book in my hand. So there I'd be when one of them would suddenly clap a hand to the top of their head and exclaim, 'Ya fuckin' bastard!', the fucking bastard in question having just hacked up a good-sized 'greener' and spat it over the outraged one's head. After this there would be a fight. I would then break up the fight… and on and on ad nauseam (literally).

And in the midst of this, the worst of the lot: Patrick.

Patrick had one tooth and very little hair. Think Dobby in

*Harry Potter* without the big ears (though come to think of it…). I was teaching in a mobile. The windows were caged. Quite often, Patrick would announce his arrival by jumping up on the windows and hanging there like an ape while banging the caging. He would then hop from one window to another around the mobile while his classmates cheered him on, before they grew bored and began spitting on one another again.

I was supposed to teach this lot.

*I was supposed to introduce them to Shakespeare!*

I still find it remarkable that I didn't just pack it in in those first few months. The only thing that stopped me was that I'd just taken out a mortgage. Otherwise, I would have walked.

I dreamed of gripping Patrick by the throat, of kicking his shit in, of running him down with my car and then reversing back over him. He was just… what's the word? He would sit at the back of the class by the radiator. It was one of those big box-like contraptions that blew out hot air. He would spend most classes wafting sheets of paper against the radiator, watching them stick against the grill. He could do that for a full hour. Either that or he would simply put his head down on the desk. When I approached him, he wouldn't lift his head; instead he would lift his middle finger and crook it at me and tell me to fuck off out of his life. If he did eventually lift his head, he would stare dully at me. Unhinged, that's the word. There seemed to be nothing going on behind that boy's eyes except pure violence. Summoning up the courage, I would sit down beside him and try to talk to him, explain that I was his teacher and that I was paid to try to get him through his exams. 'Fuck – you stink!' he would growl. All the while, he would be clenching and unclenching his fists. 'What are you looking at me like that for?' he would say. 'What – you like wee boys, you queer perv? You want me to suck your dick?' There was a venom and a hate that froze me. I wasn't blind; I've read enough psychology to know that this was self-hate, too, a rancid self-loathing which might make him capable of anything. Knowing this, though, wasn't going to do him or me any good. I wasn't a counsellor; I was a teacher. All I could do was report his behaviour. Sometimes he was suspended. Then he was back and it was the same absolutely unhinged, malevolent, terrifying shit all over again. Each time he walked through my door, my heart sank and my skin prickled with goosebumps. He was a hand grenade and even the worst head-bangers in the class knew to steer well clear.

Then I was in a pub one night. I was with some friends, standing at the bar, and there was a guy at the other end who kept looking at me. Hey-ho, I thought, you're barking up the wrong tree, mate. Then he came up to me. He was an older guy with this big, untidy beard and he was drunk. 'You teach Patrick _____, don't you? I've seen you at the school.' Wary, I said I did. He introduced himself to me and then proceeded to tell me this story about Patrick. Now, how this guy came by this story, I don't know. He might have been a relation of Patrick's, but I suspected he had something to do with social services. If so, he was breaching a lot of rules. But, as I said, he was drunk. Maybe Patrick's story was why he was drunk.

Patrick lived with his aunt – how this was, why this was, I have no idea – but I say 'lived' in the loosest sense of the word. Patrick was locked in a bedroom. Well, not so much a bedroom, just a room, and 'locked' is the wrong word too. What the aunt did was balance a cup on the handle of the door so that if Patrick tried to get out then the cup would fall and smash on the floor (the floor being bare concrete, of course). The aunt didn't want to be disturbed, you see, because she was addicted to butane. She inhaled the gas from canisters of fluid, the kind you refill lighters with. She bought six-packs of this stuff – I mean, what the fuck? – and spent most of her days getting dangerously, hideously shit-faced. Anyway, if that isn't surreal enough, Patrick had a friend: a mouse that lived amongst the chip papers, crisp packets and pizza boxes that littered his excuse for a room. According to the beardy drunk guy, Patrick and the mouse became quite fond of one another. But this friendship ended abruptly the night that Auntie burst in and discovered Mr Mouse. Completely out of her tree, she demanded that Patrick hold the little rodent up by its tail. Terrified, Patrick complied. Then Miss Shit-Faced lit a match and napalmed Mr Mouse with a squirt from a can from her six-pack of lighter fluid.

As you do.

How the other half lives, what? Or doesn't live. How this guy came by this story, as I say, I'll never know. All I do know is that Patrick abruptly disappeared from our rolls toward the end of that teaching year. A few years later, he was in the local paper for breaking and entering. He did time.

Then some months back, he walked past me while pushing a pram. He gave no indication as to whether he recognised me or not. Regardless, it seems he's trying to construct some life for himself. In his head, I hope he makes it out of that room. I wish him all the luck in the world with that. Maybe I'll wish Corey the same someday.

Or maybe not.

# 6 FEBRUARY

Took it easy today and dusted off my grammar book. It's a handy number. Photocopy a few exercises out of it – homophones, antonyms and synonyms, commas, semi-colons – give those out to the classes, tell them they can't write on the photocopied sheet and must write the full passages out in their notebooks before they fill in the answers. Get their heads down, while I get on with some marking. Easy money. Ha!

I remember a colleague who swore the three most important words in the teacher's lexicon were 'Write it out'. When computers entered the equation it became 'Type it out'.

The exercises are useful, grammatically speaking. But I don't pretend it's teaching. Teaching – and learning – is discussion, the teasing out of ideas, questioning, roleplay. There's none of that shit going on when I open my old friend the grammar book. Yet, if anybody pops their head round the door, they see a class of boys and girls scribbling away, quiet as mice. For all intents and purposes there appears to be teaching and learning going on. I repeat: there isn't. There's just a teacher getting on with their marking. Sometimes, oftentimes, I'll have classes to prepare when I pull this stroke. Then again, sometimes I'm just tired or hacked off, and I set those grammar exercises and mentally put my feet up.

Then there are the classes for whom those grammar exercises are the only thing that works. Those or just reading from a novel. There are many classes like that where discussion, the teasing out of ideas, questioning, roleplay – as I say, teaching and learning – are just such a headache that it's not worth it. Instead, you get them sat down quickly, get their books out quickly, get them writing quickly or reading quickly. You'll notice the operative word there. Classes like these can go the whole year without any real teaching or learning happening. Yet their books will be full. They might even be neat. More than that, they'll even be marked with pithy little comments in the margins such as '"No" as in "*No*, I won't", "know" as in "I *know* the answer". KNOW the difference.' What's more – and this is the real kicker – a pound to a penny these pupils will, if not enjoy, then appreciate this work. They appreciate its discipline; they appreciate that they'll know exactly what they'll be doing in the class. There's no bullshit: it's books out, heads down.

And, of course, the above is how kids used to be taught, the only difference being if you lifted your head fifty years ago you got a blackboard duster thrown at it, or the teacher's shoe, or whatever was handy.

Now I'm not allowed to do those things. With a difficult class, my only weapon is my grammar book.

Or a video.

Or an audio book.

Audio books are very good. To continue the weaponry metaphor, audio books are howitzers; shit, they're fucking aircraft carriers! Highly recommended, especially – *especially!* – if the book itself is boring. That way we can all have a little nap. I have an audio book of *Of Mice and Men*. I treasure it and keep it in a special, secret place, wrapped in velvet. All respect to John Steinbeck, but *Of Mice and Men* has to be the most boring novel ever written. There's Jane Austen and Henry James novels that come close but, really... to think that people once read *Of Mice and Men* for pleasure. To think there have been so many film adaptations of it, so many stage versions of this mawkish, plodding melodrama – in the name of sweet Christ, why? The only thing I can say in its favour is that it's short. It's been on the GCSE syllabus for ever, and will probably continue to be because teachers have a load of notes on it and they'd be loath to burn them and have to draw up new notes on a better novel. Then again, as I've said, every novel since William Caxton got his bright idea is better than *Of Mice and Men*.

But very few of them come in audio book form. And this is a very special audio book. Oh, it has saved me many times! Even the most recalcitrant head-banger is putty in my hands if I unleash the power of this audio book. There they are, bouncing in through the door, flinging their bag halfway across the room, calling such-and-such a wanker, such-and-such a slut, plonking themselves in their seat, legs akimbo, arms folded, looking at me with a big shit-eating smile: 'Whaddya got, fuck-face?' that smile says. But I'm smiling too. An evil smile…

I press play.

The look on their face, like I've turned over a royal flush to their full house; like I've led them by the hand to the very gates of Hell itself.

It's like swinging a gold watch on a chain. 'Your eyes are heavy, you are feeling very sleepy…' Five minutes later and the whole class are in a state of extreme stupor, like in one of those films where an army helicopter passes overhead and sprays some midwestern American town with nerve agent.

Brilliant, wha?

But the plan is I play a chapter of the audio each class. At the end of each session, the pupils would be wakened (provided I am awake). When they've wiped the drool from their chins and examined the indents of their sleeves on the side of their faces, they are handed a worksheet of multiple-choice questions to check that some of the story has penetrated their dream state. Even if it hasn't, it will take them about two minutes to copy answers in form-class the next day from someone who has somehow managed to keep their eyes open. (There's always one such insomniac.) That way, I can act delighted and praise their studiousness and gave them all a tick for homework done. (Don't want people not doing their homework. If that happens, I have to keep them behind at lunch and I miss my dinner.)

After completing the audio book, we watch the video. Ha, the fun just never stops. The video contains the most laughable piece of miscasting I've ever witnessed in the form of John Malkovich as Lennie. Now, I hadn't realised Malkovich was so tall, and he tries his best to catch the lumbering gait of the bearlike man-child Lennie, but he finds it almost impossible to play dumb. Maybe he should find it easy – maybe he isn't as cerebral as he looks, or as he pretends in so many of his roles – but let's just say Lennie Small isn't his finest hour. (A note to Hollywood producers: if you want to inflict another adaptation of *Of Mice and Men* on the world, Liam Neeson would be perfect for Lennie. He's a huge bastard and has no problem whatsoever playing dumb.)

After the video, students will then take verbatim notes on the novel's themes, characters, symbolism, politics and so on from the overhead projector (provided there isn't too much glare on the whiteboard thanks to the missing blinds and curtains). Then they will be set a question for coursework. This is where most of my work is done. I will mark this illiterate scrawl thoroughly, providing linking passages, sometimes writing entire paragraphs and usually a decent conclusion eulogising Steinbeck's place in the great pantheon of hypocritical Yankie bullshitters and snake-oil salesmen. The pupils will then type up the redraft.

Job done; minimal discussion or disruption necessary. Everybody's happy.

And none the wiser.
But well rested.

# 7 FEBRUARY

I gave Angela her essay back today. As expected, we could all have stood round her and warmed our hands off her face. But she was pleased. Then I realised something: this was the first piece of work Angela had done since Davina had been moved up a class. Is this what Angela could do when she wasn't distracted and could fully focus on a task? Well, that's now a moot point. Because Davina's back. She wanted to be moved down again to be with her best friend. Her parents actually came in to see the Principal and ask that Davina be demoted. She was only in the new class a week. Couldn't they have tried to persuade her to stick it out a little while longer? Couldn't they have impressed upon her that her studies must come first, that in another ten or twenty years Angela will probably be nothing but a memory?

Or maybe friendship is more important?

What if Davina does well in her GCSEs in a few years' time but has no one to celebrate with? Maybe that's a little extreme. But I see so many unhappy children these days. More than I used to, I'm sure of that. I see more kids sitting on their own. Mental health issues, self-harming: all on the rise. The Office for National Statistics' latest findings show that the number of teenage suicides in England and Wales increased 67 per cent between 2010 and 2017. According to Unicef, in 2017 Ireland had the fourth highest teen suicide rate in the EU/OECD region. Fuck, I vaguely remember how difficult it was to be a teenager – does anybody really like me? Is my dick going to get any bigger? Now they knock on Facebook and Instagram and Snapchat and see what a good time everyone else is having, or pretending to have. Boys surf porn, and watch the sexual gymnastics of someone with a phallus the size of a French loaf, and then look down at their own sorry member.

In 2016, a Middlesex University study of children aged eleven to sixteen found that 48 per cent had seen pornography online. Of this group, the vast majority – 94 per cent – had seen such material by age fourteen, with 60 per cent of children having first watched it in their own homes. A 2019 Irish study in the journal *Porn Studies* (yep, that's its name. And I don't subscribe to it, by the way) found that 52 per cent of boys started using pornography for masturbation at the age of thirteen or under. Think about that. Think about what's going on in their heads at such a formative age while they watch this stuff. What does it tell them about girls? What are they thinking about on a first date – should we kiss first or go straight to the blow-job? Does she do anal? Maybe that's more exaggeration, but I would suggest this pornographic fixation will do nothing to curtail incidents of rape or sexual harassment, no matter how many talks Love For Life gives. Of girls and porn? I'm not getting into that, but I think it's safe to say it doesn't help them feel any better about themselves. I set an essay for a group of fifth years last year entitled 'Life is harder for young people than it has ever been'. Every girl in the class wrote about body/self-image. Every girl. Kate wrote:

Social media plays a big part in our lives nowadays since almost everyone has a phone. Young people use snapchat, Instagram, facebook etc … These platforms are filled with models and people who have had plastic surgery or where their pictures have been photo-shopped. Young people view these images and then look at themselves and wonder why they don't look like that and start to judge themselves and their every little flaw. Often young people will then fixate on their appearance and cover themselves in make-up and go on diets or join a gym. This can often lead to depression, anorexia and other mental illnesses and eating disorders and, worst of all, suicide.

Imogen wrote this:

Most young people feel bad about their bodies and much of this is because of the internet. All of those perfect bodies on the internet! Yet, this is mostly photo-shopping. But even when we know that images have been photo-shopped there is still the desire to look like this. We all have to live up to this. Things like diet suppressions [*sic*] and diet lollipops are advertised beside these images and these adverts should be banned. How many young people are happy with how they look when they surf social media or watch television like 'Love Island'? We know it is fake so why do we want to be fake too?

All of the girls lambasted false ideals of womanhood and all saw them for the tyranny they were. However, the mere fact that so many had concentrated on this issue suggested they felt trapped, terrified even, by those images of 'beauty' and 'perfection' they were constantly bombarded with. Boys feel this pressure too, but I don't think it's anything to what girls feel. What are we going to do about it? For instance, how is the curriculum addressing this crisis? And that's the word: crisis. (On the other hand, Thomas had an interesting take on those forces which cause undue stress for young people: 'Everyone talks about global warming and the seas getting higher and ice-bergs melting and deforestation of forests even though most of the trees that would save us are being chopped down for school exercise books because of all the homework we get.')

So if Angela and Davina are back together again, I'm not going to shake my head and tut. A few years ago, I would have. Not now. Kids need as many friends as they can get to navigate the increasingly murky waters of adolescence; they need real physical friendship, rather than a cyber-buddy. Talking together, laughing together, hugs, doing each other's hair (which is what Angela and Davina engage in a lot of the time)... I'm not going to knock any of that.

Anyway, back to Angela's story. I praise it and then put the last paragraph on the board.

> We walked into my house and it was clean, warm and tidy. I told her to hop into the shower and get washed so that's what she did. She walked into the living room in a white robe and asked where my daughter was and I said she will be home soon then she sat down so I walked into the kitchen and got my homemade tomado soop and spict it to make her sleepy. As soon as I handed her it she ate it like there was no tomorrow. She fell asleep on the couch and I walked up to her and stabbed her to death and then took a picture of the body. I dressed her up a lay her next to the other bodys.

I asked Angela why she wrote that the house was 'clean, warm and tidy'. Angela said that if the house was that way – and not a tip – then the girl would feel more at ease. We decided that we needed to draw that out some more. We also decided that we needed to hear the sarcastic voice of the killer more and that there should be some dialogue. We also should get rid of all those 'walked' (along with 'went' and 'got', two of the laziest words in the English language). Similarly, some temporal clauses were needed, such as 'After that...' 'Next thing...' 'Two minutes later...' Also, paragraphs. We needed more of them. For some reason, kids are always loath to use up the space on their pages. Finally, we got to the big line about photographing the body. I asked Angela where she got that from.

'Because he would do that, wouldn't he?' she said.

'Why?' I asked.

'Because he's a sicko,' someone else interjected.

'I know!' says Cathal. 'He wouldn't photograph them. He'd put them on a chair and take off all their clothes, and video the whole thing on his phone, with them naked and all.' Cathal was getting excited and making involuntary masturbatory movements. This was literally getting out of hand.

'Why?' I asked Angela again.

'So when he looked at the photo he could remember how smart he was – that he could kill somebody like this and nobody caught him.'

I'll have to keep an eye on Angela.

Anyway, we put together the following:

We entered my house and it was clean, neat and tidy and she was impressed. She smiled for the first time and I saw her becoming more relaxed. This was going to be easy.

I told her to hop into the shower. 'First on the left up the stairs', I told her. 'Take your time'. She bloody well did too. Half an hour later she walks into my living-room like she was a movie star in my white robe. The cheek of her!

'I hope you don't mind', she said.

'Oh no, not at all', I said through gritted teeth.

'Where's your daughter?'

'Oh, she must have popped out', I told her. 'She'll be home soon. Here, have a seat and I'll get you something to eat'.

She curled up on the sofa beside Sappho. [Sappho being the killer's cat.]

In the kitchen, I spiked my home-made tomato soup with sleeping tablets. She had no suspicions and ate it like there was no tomorrow, not knowing there was no tomorrow.

Five minutes later, she was dead to the world. Literally, ha! I took the picture of the body. Why? It makes me feel good. An album of memories, things to look back on when I'm old and grey to prove I was smarter than them, all them coppers and do-gooders.

I dressed her and lay her down with the other bodies.

If you ask me, that's pretty good, and 10P thought so too.

# 8 FEBRUARY

It was Corey wot done it!

Flooded the toilets.

Told ya!

As I said, I don't teach him any more, but I'd come across him the previous day. I went into the computer suite to photocopy some stuff. Corey's class were in there and, surprise, an irate teacher was standing over him. It seems the class had to do some kind of multiple-choice test on the computer. Foolishly, as the teacher admitted in retrospect, she had said that once the pupils had finished the test they could go on to the internet and play a game or whatever. The test should have taken up to half an hour which would give them ten minutes or so to fool around. Fair enough, but two minutes into the test the teacher looked around and there was Corey already playing a game.

'What are you doing?' she asked him. 'Get on with your test!'

'I've finished,' he says.

And, technically, he *had* finished. He had simply scrolled

through the test as quickly as possible, ticking any random box as he went along.

'You haven't done the test properly, Corey,' said the teacher. 'I want you to go back and do it properly.'

'I've finished,' he says. 'You said once we'd finished, we could play a game.'

The teacher was in a bind. Corey was in the right. He was in the wrong, but he was in the right. There was also the possibility that he's slightly autistic along with everything else that's going on in his head. With autistic students, you absolutely have to watch what you say when giving instructions. I had one notorious example of it in my experience. I once asked a first-year class to 'back' their books for the next day. Y'know, get some wallpaper or some gift paper or clingfilm, or anything really, and cover their books. It's de rigueur in primary school but not so much in secondary school. I like to get them to do it because I think it suggests that continuation with primary school and it's also sending the message that they should take pride in their book and what's inside it. Anyway, they were sent off to back their books. Next day, I'm checking them and this little fella – can't remember his name – hadn't put a cover on his book. Or so I thought. Until I turned it over and was looking at this green diamond wallpaper. He had 'backed' the back of his book with this ugly wallpaper. Just the back, mind, not the front. I had told him to 'back' his book and he had literally done just that. And it was the neatest job you ever saw. I mean, it must have taken him fucking ages. Furthermore, he wasn't taking the piss. He was simply very autistic. So autistic that if I had accused him of taking the piss, he would have asked me where he should take the piss to.

Corey, though, would have known exactly what I meant by taking the piss.

The teacher crossed to where I was standing by the photocopier. Her face was white with anger, a vein thick as a Doc Marten bootlace pulsing by the side of her forehead. She asked for my advice.

'Kick his fuck in!' I told her.

I don't know what she did in the end. Now he's suspended and is being referred to the Board of Governors for possible exclusion. But not just for the toilets. No, it seems he threw a bin at the Principal. I don't know the details, but I suspect that when confronted with such an impugnation of his unimpeachable character, he responded the only way he knew: by fucking said rubbish receptacle at his accuser. Note that this wasn't some little wastepaper bin but one of those four-foot-high barrel-like corridor bins. I can just picture him, standing astride the world like Samson before the Philistines, bin juice running down the back of his neck. Anyway, he's suspended, along with another pupil who was running in the concourse and knocked over a pregnant teacher.

Ah, the fun just never stops!

All this going on and I check my pigeon-hole. It's full to the throat. My secret Santa's still in there: a Stephen Fry novel. Why the hell anyone thinks I would want to read a novel by Stephen Fry, I really don't know. Somebody has got me all wrong. Honestly, I'd rather eat my own shit than read a book by that child of the Entitlement. Or somebody else's shit. Come to think of it, I'd rather eat Stephen's Fry's shit than read one of his books. But besides the Fry and the other rubbish, there's a booklet in my pigeon-hole from the Department for Education entitled 'Putting Care into Education'.

It's full of advice about how to deal with children with problems. For instance, here it is on empathy:

> To understand the child's needs we have to put ourselves in their shoes and show them that we 'get it'. For example, 'I know that these spellings are hard for you to remember', 'I get it that it's hard for you to come to school every day'. Empathy allows a child to feel their feelings and encourages the release of grief, fear and rage behind emotional and behavioural problems. Try to empathise with a child before disciplining and throughout the employment of disciplinary measures (e.g. consequences). It is vital that you remain genuinely empathetic, not flippant, mocking or sarcastic. Sarcasm seriously undermines trust and makes a child feel not valued.

Sounds brilliant. I wouldn't argue with a word. But I would also argue that whoever wrote this has never spent a day, or any sustained period of time, at least, in a classroom. Think of the teacher conducting that computer test. Think of the twenty or so other children in the class. What about their shoes? More importantly, what about inspectors when they look at a school's exam results and it is explained to them that, oh yes, well, you see, Corey was in that class, and his behaviour took up so much teaching time and we made such an effort to empathise with him and walk a mile in his moccasins that, well, the curriculum couldn't quite be covered in the depth that was necessary, hence the poor results.

Will they 'get it'?

Will they fuck!

# 11 FEBRUARY

There was a short meeting in the staffroom at the end of the day to tell us that things were bad but that we should take this opportunity to look on the bright side for as long as we could, because they were going to get a hell of a lot worse – and y'know all those people visiting food banks and railing against the injustices of Universal Credit? Well, that could be us if we didn't win the lottery in the next couple of months.

The Principal explained that the Education Authority was £1.1 billion in debt. She said that our school itself was running at a debt of £350k a year, although she would be able to post a debt of £310k for the present year because she had saved £40k on sub cover, thus explaining why I'm not getting any free classes any more. When I say free classes, by the way, this doesn't mean I just put my feet up and enjoy a few luxuriant farts; free classes, or non-teaching periods, are meant to be time when I can prepare classes, get some marking done or catch up with a pupil for a little one-on-one 'empathy' time (where I put the care into education, to borrow the phraseology). But all that's out the window in this new dawn of cash-strapped pedagogy.

Anyway, the Principal wanted to reassure staff that she would fight tooth and nail to prevent redundancies. Safe to say, I left the meeting feeling about as secure in my employment as a Bible salesman in Kabul.

Then again, if I lose my job, maybe it will force me to do something else with my life. I've argued time out of number with colleagues that twenty years should be the lifespan of the job. I've done twenty-five. I could have committed a double murder and been out by now. After twenty years I think you're simply going through the motions. Yes, you have experience, and that counts for a lot, but kids need a lot more; they need energy, they need inspiration, they need somebody at the front of the room talking shite and actually believing it, telling them they can change the world. As Yeats said, 'Education is not the filling of a pail, but the lighting of a fire.'

I feel like I'm kicking over the embers.

I'm tired. I'm tired in my bones, I'm tired in my head. I've had successes. I actually have had kids who bought me a card when they were leaving to say that I made a difference to them. I remember filling up at a garage one night and this guy came running across the forecourt. I thought I was about to be mugged before this man stuck out his hand to shake mine. He said that I taught his son, Dermot, and that Dermot had decided to be a teacher because of me. I told this deluded father he should be slapping the jaws off me, rather than shaking my hand, but I don't think I've ever been more choked. When I left my previous school, the GCSE class I taught achieved the best results ever recorded in the school. My God, but that was a class! I fought with them and fought with them, slugged it out day after day to get the best work they were capable of. At one point I went on strike. We had completed the coursework and they thought they could just coast toward the exam. I argued that now was the time to put in the real work. They weren't having it. They were a bolshy bunch of bastards, full of personality, full of fight. But so was I, back then. In so many words, I told them to go fuck themselves. Then I went on strike.

The strike wasn't some cunning plan on my part, some well-thought-out ploy. Truth was, I was huffing. Not bluffing, but huffing, sulking – taking my ball back and going home. I took it personally that they weren't as fired up as I was. (Just to note, it's always a bad idea to take this stuff personally.) But why was I so fired up? This was my chance to prove a point. The boys in this class were all 'failures'. They had failed to get into the grammar school at the other end of town. This when they were fourteen, not eleven as in the eleven-plus system. Condemning the eleven-plus as 'pernicious', the Educational District where I was then teaching had pushed back the age of grammar school entry to fourteen. Therefore, all pupils sat an exam at the end of their third year (Year 10). I have no doubt the intention was good. I've seen the effects of the eleven-plus, or the Transfer Test as it's called now: very young children almost traumatised by the pressure. To give kids three more years before they go through that trauma, when they are hopefully more mature and able to handle the pressure that little bit better; that should be a good idea. However, there are always casualties, no matter how good the idea might seem (think of those Trojans: 'Hey, man, open the gates, that is one cool horse!'). This class of mine, they were the casualties. At least with the eleven-plus, kids who were disappointed moved to a new school even if it wasn't the school of their choice; a new school where there would be new teachers, new choices and second chances. But in that area, those who failed the exam and weren't going to the grammar school stayed in their present school and sat their GCSEs.

*Whoopee-fucking-woo!*

In a more enlightened country, these children would have been steered into vocational courses where they could get proper training as electricians, plumbers, car mechanics, joiners and so on. Instead, they came back in Year 11 in the exact same uniform to do the exact same shit, as if the exam had never happened. Can you imagine how disaffected they were? Believe me, disaffected is too polite a word. Disaffected is a euphemism that knocks all other euphemisms into a cocked fucking hat. I mean, would you listen to the specky fuck-head cunt at the front of the room telling you you weren't a failure, that you could get GCSEs, that you just had to knuckle down and apply yourself – this after you had just failed the biggest exam of your life? I know I wouldn't. Then again, I was that specky fuck-head cunt at the front of the room, and the thing was... I meant it! This was the point I wanted to prove – that we would show those grammar school shitheads and in so doing we would stick it to the system.

*Oh, the vanity of youth!*

My youth, by the way, not theirs.

So we spent Year 11 getting the coursework done. Hercules would have given up – he never had to deal with as much shit as this when he was dunging out the Augean Stables – but we got there in the end and some of the work was decent enough to make me quietly (very quietly) optimistic about the following year. Year 12 was going to be exam preparation, past papers for the most part.

Except they quit.

So I quit.

When they came into class, I didn't even look at them. I let them just sit there and talk and shout and fart and fire things at one another. A couple of times – more than a couple of times – the teacher in the room next door came in to ask what the hell was going on. And this went on for ages until one miraculous class – and I don't use that adjective lightly – everything went dead quiet. There wasn't a sound. Even they were pissed off with the chaos. I looked at them for the first time in about a month. 'Can we get on with this?' I asked them.

So we got on with it. We really got on with it. And getting on with it doesn't mean making speeches, by the way, or going out to talk to these kids' drug-addled mothers, or trying to stop them getting involved in gangs, or finding a new resolve, or rising to our strengths after Emilio or Pedro or Carlos gets shot in a drive-by. It isn't telling them to stand on desks and shout 'Captain! My captain!' (There was a lot of standing on desks in our school but nobody was quoting Walt Whitman while they punched a hole in the ceiling-tiles.) Neither was it being charmed by some fat bloke called Hector who teaches when he feels like it and who wraps his big juicy lips around compound words like 'cunt-struck'. In *The History Boys* this means an addiction to sex; in our school it meant being struck by a cunt, often repeatedly. No, getting on with it meant learning that 'soldier' wasn't spelt 'soilder'; that you're not allowed to use 'cause', that it's 'because'; that it's not 'Where of you bin?' it's 'Where have you been?' It's teaching people to quote from a text and use quotation marks and follow this up with 'This line suggests' or 'This line illustrates' rather than 'Like this kind of shows me' or 'What I think yer man means is'. It's the nuts and bolts of proper English, repeated ad nauseam until you feel like hurling someone out the window or they want to do the same to you. There's nothing Hollywood about it. It's a grind. There is no End of Act Two 'All is Lost' moment, because at every moment all seems lost – or put down somewhere where you can't fucking find it.

So we got the prep done. They sat the exam. To remind you, the expectation was that a few of these boys would get Cs and the rest would fail. That was the benchmark from previous years. That was what the other classes in the school got that year.

What did we get?

Every single one of those stroppy, recalcitrant, infuriating, beautiful motherfuckers passed!

Every single one of them. There was one A, a handful of Bs and the rest got Cs.

Best English GCSEs ever recorded by a class in the school!

One particular boy, Ciaran, passed his GCSE with a B. Everything was a joke to Ciaran, and he had to make it a joke, to laugh it off, because he couldn't do anything. At least, that's what he believed. He wrote long Faulknerian sentences: no full stops, no paragraphs, just one long sentence with no sense of an ending. Faulkner had the excuse of being drunk and a Nobel laureate. Ciaran had no excuse other than that he was crap at English. But by the time he sat the exam he'd put in a full stop like he was planting a flag, begin a new paragraph like he was sighting a spirit-level and about to lay a new line of bricks. And he got a B! He deserved every plaudit. His grade was a testament to his character. He sweated blood for that result. And so did I.

But... I couldn't do it now.

I couldn't.

I've run into Ciaran a few times since he left school. He's one of the nicest guys you could meet. He'd ask me how I was, and I'd ask him how he was, and how such-and-such was doing and so on. The last time I spoke to him was when my mother and I were picking out a headstone for my father's grave. I kid you not. Ciaran's a stone mason; that's the family business. He shook my mother's hand, he shook my hand, and said he was sorry for our trouble. Then we picked a stone. Then we picked something to write on it and there I was leaning over Ciaran's shoulder making sure he got the spelling right. We had a laugh at that; me and this bearded man who was now in his thirties. And suddenly I was winded, wounded, by an irrevocable sense of loss. On a drab wet September afternoon, in this dingy office with a paraffin heater, and a smell of damp, and a window looking out into a shadowy room where grey and black and marble headstones were propped against the walls like gap teeth, I felt the loss of my father more keenly than at any other time in the weeks since his death. Or maybe it was the loss of all those years since I had been Ciaran's teacher. Suddenly, I felt my age, that I was not the same man who had taught Ciaran. There's the title of that Greene story, *A Burnt-Out Case*. Well, that was me. That was how I felt. Of course, I wasn't in the greatest place at the time. My father had been diagnosed with cancer in June; he died in August. Those two months had exhausted our family emotionally and physically. By the end, my father was on ketamine to deal with the pain, drool running from his nose and his mouth. The carers – blessed people whose diligence and kindness I will never forget – would come in and roll him over on the orthopaedic bed in the living room to change his nappy. I couldn't get that out of my head. This was my father, goddammit!

I didn't break down in front of Ciaran. That would have been uncalled for, to see his old teacher in bits. That would have been embarrassing. No, there was too much of the teacher still left in me to let that happen. But I cried in the car after I'd dropped my mother home. With the September rain belting off the windscreen, I cried for her, I cried for my father, and I cried for myself and for all those years I was never getting back again.

Time is a river.

Maybe I'm ready for redundancy.

# 12 FEBRUARY

## SCENE ONE

*Cue music: something soft yet transcendent such as Rachmaninoff's 'Rhapsody on a Theme of Paganini'.*

*The classroom could do with a lick of paint. There are no curtains or blinds on the window. Neither is there an interactive whiteboard. There isn't even a DVD player. But there is... unless my eyes are deceiving me... no, it definitely is – it's even written in faded capitals around the thing – a glory hole!*

*Come to think of it, though, considering the general state of the room, this glory hole is the only indication we are in a 21st-century learning environment rather than a Dickensian one.*

*MR CHIPOLATA – hereon known as Mr Chip – sits behind his desk. A rakish, debonair, cultured, worldly wise and handsome man with the gravitas of an Abe Lincoln, Mr Chip is loved and gives love in equal measure. He is lost in his latest plan to end world hunger as 8D enter his room.*

*CUT MUSIC very abruptly, as if it had been ripped from a turntable.*

*MR CHIP – OK, 8D, books out, homeworks out.*

*Muffled expostulations of 'Did we have homework?'*

*MR CHIP – But first I want to see the homework diaries of Jason, Louis, Cora, Chantelle and Sandy. Your homework diaries were all to be signed by someone at home after you didn't do the last homework. Jason?*

*With a tremendous sigh, moving like he's carrying someone in a fireman's lift, Jason comes forward with his homework diary, which has been signed.*

*MR CHIP – Good man. Louis?*

*LOUIS – My ma was busy.*

*MR CHIP – I wrote that note in your diary three days ago, Louis. Your mother was busy for three days?*

*LOUIS – I've done my homework for today.*

*MR CHIP – But you didn't do it for the last day, hence the note in your homework diary. I told you if you didn't get that signed then you would receive another X. So that's two Xs you have now. Another one and you're on after-school detention.*

*LOUIS – That's not fair, I've done my homework for the day. That's so crap!*

*MR CHIP – Watch your mouth, Louis.*

*LOUIS – But it is!*

*MR CHIP – Do you want this other X now or are you going to accept what I'm telling you?*

*Louis shuts up.*

*MR CHIP – Cora?*

*CORA – I forgot my homework diary.*

*MR CHIP – But you keep it in your blazer pocket.*

*CORA – I know, but I took it out to check what homework I had and forgot to put it back in. But I did get it signed.*

*MR CHIP – I'm sorry, Cora, but I need to see the homework diary and I need to see it signed. That's another X you've got, too. Chantelle?*

*CHANTELLE – I forgot mine too.*

*MR CHIP – Your homework diary?*

*CHANTELLE – Yeah.*

*MR CHIP – Did you get it signed?*

*CHANTELLE – Yeah.*

*MR CHIP – Well, that's all right then.*

*CHANTELLE – Really?*

*MR CHIP – No, not really. That's three Xs you've got. You are now on after-school detention.*

*CHANTELLE – Aw – when?*

*MR CHIP – I haven't decided, but you can be sure I'll let you know. Sandy?*

*Head down, mournful, Sandy gets up from her seat and comes forward with a jotter and a pen.*

*MR CHIP – What's this, Sandy?*

*SANDY – I've lost my homework diary. Could you write the note again in this and I'll get my mammy to sign it?*

*MR CHIP – No, I won't write the note again, Sandy. I recommend that you have another look for your diary. In the meantime, that's another X.*

*A downcast Sandy returns to her seat, her cunning plan thwarted. In the meantime, the rest of the class are becoming restless.*

MR CHIP – *Right, 8D, that's it, schtum! OK, I want to see everyone's homework for today open on their desks. That means open to the page of the homework so that I can walk round quickly and see that it's done. Not just the book out on the desk, right? That includes you, Emily, and you, Damien.*

EMILY – *I forgot my book.*

MR CHIP – *That's an X.*

EMILY – *But I did my homework, I swear.*

MR CHIP – *Why would you do your homework and not put it in your bag? Do you check your timetable every night for the next day?*

EMILY – *Yeah.*

MR CHIP – *So how come?*

EMILY – *Don't know.*

MR CHIP – *OK, get your diary out till I write a note home, which you need to get signed for the next day. John, where's your exercise book?*

JOHN – *Left it at home. Just forgot to put it in my bag after I finished my homework.*

Mr CHIP – *X!*

JOHN – *But I did!*

MR CHIP – *You mean you didn't?*

JOHN – *Wha?*

MR CHIP – *Put it in your bag?*

JOHN – *Yeah.*

*MR CHIP – Get your diary out.*
*JOHN – I forgot it.*

Aw, fuck, I give up! Trying to liven up the unrelieved tedium of what it is to set homework with a class like 8D, and the above is pretty much verbatim – putting it in script format, dressing it up as an epic poem, using Burrough's cut-up method – you can't polish this turd or even roll it in glitter. Finally, finally, after some more of this amusing back and forth, I looked at my watch. It was 11:39. The bell had sounded for the beginning of class at 11:15. I had spent twenty-four minutes on this crap. That left eleven minutes of class. Note, I hadn't corrected the homework or heard anyone's homework. I was simply finding out who had got their diary signed after the previous missed homework and writing notes in the diaries of those who hadn't done the present homework, which in a few instances meant writing a note to be signed under the previous note which hadn't been signed.

Aaaahhhh!

The school has a homework policy: at least one homework to be set each week for every subject. With some classes that's OK. There are some classes where the majority of pupils are motivated and it's only a few lags who present a problem with homework. But if it's only a few, that is manageable. If you have the energy, you might even be able to work up a head of steam to shout at them, and ask them what the bloody hell they think they're going to bloody make of their lives if they can't do a simple bloody homework.

But with classes like 8D…

And the worth of these homeworks? Kids don't like doing them, teachers don't like marking them. If a teacher has any sense, the odd tick will serve as marking. To my mind, homework only becomes valuable if someone at home is going to sit down and go through an exercise with a child. If homework can provide that sort of framework between home and school then it must be worthwhile. Then again, against that we look at twenty-four wasted minutes of teaching time, over two-thirds of the class.

Does more homework equal greater achievement? There's the Organisation for Economic Co-operation and Development (OECD) PISA report that showed that Spanish fifteen-year-olds spend more time on homework than most, at nearly eight hours a week compared to an OECD average of nearly six. However, Spanish students are in the bottom half of PISA rankings, suggesting that spending more time doing homework doesn't always translate into higher student achievement. The report argued that children get to a point of oversaturation and that the drawbacks of a heavy workload include boredom, burnout, increased stress, lack of sleep and less time for family and extracurricular activities.

Then, as I say, there's 8D. Not much chance of oversaturation or burnout there. Not much sleep being lost either. In reality, it is just a complete waste of time.

And we ask: why do we really set these homeworks?

Here's why – because they are a fall-back, stupid, that's why; they are a first line of defence. That's why they are set.

Without them, a teacher is exposed and naked, because in any general meeting with the parents of kids who are causing a bit of bother, a pound to a penny, the first thing the parent will say is, 'He/she never seems to have any homework'; i.e. if my son/daughter has decided to set off a fire extinguisher or tried to rearrange someone's face, it's because they're not being sufficiently engaged in their studies, i.e. it's not their fault, it's the school's for not working them hard enough.

Hence, homework.

# 14 FEBRUARY

Valentine's Day and love is not in the air.

'P\*ki cunt!'

This from Eamonn. At least I thought that was what he said. I was on bus duty. Eamonn was about to board a bus when he turned and shouted what sounded like 'P\*ki cunt' at a fella standing on the grass bank beside the buses. This wasn't one I could tactically ignore. Swearing in general I will ignore when I can. As you've already figured out, I like the odd swear myself. But this wasn't just swearing. The school has a strong anti-racism policy which I happen to strongly agree with.

Eamonn's a bit of a bollix. He's ADHD (attention deficit hyperactivity disorder) and when he takes his tablets he's a nice guy. On the other hand, when for some reason he doesn't, he comes into school with his eyes shining and his big gangly frame going in three or four different directions at once. In other words, it's easy to spot when he hasn't taken his tablets. Unmedicated, he's a… Shall I repeat myself?

The only way I've found to assuage him is to let him go

on his phone if he's finished some bare minimum of work. That's against school rules. Pupils aren't allowed phones out during class. Then again, it's against school rules to disrupt everyone's education and Eamonn seems to get away with that pretty regularly. So I let him go on his phone. Like a toddler playing with bricks in a corner, it keeps him quiet. He loves that phone. He was suspended before Christmas when a teacher tried to take it off him. It seems he went complete batshit. I can believe it. Why anyone would be foolish enough to do that I have no idea. I would sooner prise a bag of chips from a starving tramp or a full-frontal of Maggie Thatcher from a horny Tory than I would take Eamonn's phone off him.

So I walk over to the guy I thought Eamonn had been shouting at. He had olive skin although, truth be told, it wasn't as olive as Eamonn's, who has some Italian blood in his veins. 'Did Eamonn just shout at you what I think he shouted at you?' I asked.

'Aye,' says he, 'he's my friend.'

'Sorry?' I says.

'He calls me a "P*ki cunt" for a joke,' he says.

I held up a hand. 'I don't want to hear that language,' I says to him. 'Now tell me – how on earth could calling anybody that be a joke?'

''Cause I'm quarter Indian.'

I needed a moment or two. 'So he calls you that because of the animosity between Pakistanis and Indians? It's like calling a Scottish person English?'

The guy looks at me the way Farquhar had looked at me a few weeks before when he couldn't understand why he wasn't allowed to smoke in school.

What is it about me and duty?

'He's being ironic?' I continued. 'Sarcastic?'

'No,' says yer man. 'It's because when he calls me an "Indy cunt" it sounds kind of cool. So he calls me a "P*ki cunt" instead.'

I was going to respond to this and then... well, I just didn't bother.

Instead, I walked down off the bank and took up my position by the bus stop again, and looked up at the sky and tried to count the clouds, or the number of cracked paving stones on the school avenue, or the blades of grass growing between those cracks; trying to do something, in other words, that was more useful than involving myself in the lives of young people.

Children: their minds, a whole other country.

Literally so, in this case.

# 17 FEBRUARY

Animated discussion in the staffroom today.

I hate the staffroom. A load of people moaning and sighing at the same time is grand if it's an orgy (like *I* would know) but not if it's your place of work. I usually try to steer well clear but I have to check my pigeon-hole the odd time. Usually I zig-zag towards it with my head down like I'm negotiating Sniper Alley. After I've checked there's nothing in there that could possibly warrant more than two seconds' consideration, including the Fry (*especially the Fry!*), I repeat the manoeuvre in reverse, but sometimes my name gets called. I will pull up like a bullet's just zipped past my nose and then have to listen to somebody asking me about a pupil or some other shit.

The place, the staffroom, used to smell of smoke; now it smells of lentils because of the veggies microwaving their mush. I preferred the smoke. Progress, what? The non-vegetarians, meanwhile, eat their ham sandwiches out of their lunchboxes, with maybe a Penguin or a stick of Twix in there and a packet of crisps, the same as when they were pupils themselves. It's hideously, institutionally, depressing. Most people drink instant coffee from a huge jar that thirty years ago would have been stolen and packed with nails and Semtex and used to blow up policemen and soldiers. Mock-epic flare-ups occur when somebody hasn't contributed their monthly stipend to the coffee and the milk, or when they're behind in the staff lottery. Formerly, people used to contribute to pension schemes, but with wages and interest rates as they are the lottery now serves as most teachers' idea of a financial plan.

But the argument today wasn't about the coffee or the milk or the lottery. In fact, it had to do with teaching itself – mixed-ability classes. The Principal has decided to introduce mixed ability from next year. This means we do away with 'streaming' or 'setting' – top, middle and bottom classes. Pupils who can identify the difference between a Petrarchan and Shakespearean sonnet will be taught beside pupils who spell poems 'pomes'.

The debate was wide-ranging and stimulating. The Plowden Report was mentioned, and its emphasis on child-centred teaching, and how 'setting' was out of favour in the '70s but began to make a comeback in the mid-'90s. Someone said that in 1997 the then Department for Education and Employment had advised schools to consider setting pupils by ability in order to raise standards. Someone brought up Teach First and its 2009 report which concluded that all children should be taught in mixed-ability classes to boost standards and self-esteem amongst all students.

Someone else chimed in with the Saint John Fisher College's report 'Social and Academic Advantages and Disadvantages of Within-class Heterogeneous and Homogeneous Ability Grouping', which argued that high-ability students may succeed in either ability grouping style but, importantly, low-ability students experienced much greater academic achievement as a result of heterogeneous ability groups. Of course, against this there were the conclusions of Sir Michael Wilshaw, the head of Ofsted. A lot of the staff nodded at this. Wilshaw had recently stated that mixed ability can harm the more able. But no sooner was this mentioned than someone across the room waved their lunchbox and stated that Wilshaw was taken out of context and what he criticised was the lack of proper differentiated teaching methods. The debate then moved on to...

*Aye, right!*

Of course, none of the above was mentioned. 'But how could it be?' says you. 'What sad sack has any of the above floating around in their heads?' Maybe the Plowden Report, but that's about it. It's taken me a few hours of research to wade through a tiny percentage of the pros and cons of mixed ability. I could have also brought up a 2012 OECD report which analysed successes and failures in thirty-nine of the world's most developed nations and concluded that pupils streamed into ability groups tend to have lower levels of achievement. There's also Carol Ann Tomlinson's landmark book, *The Differentiated Classroom: Responding to the Needs of All Learners*, which came down on the side of mixed ability. And there'll be lots more research: library shelves groaning under the weight of it, hard drives clogged with it.

My point? Ignorance of this research didn't stop anybody talking, didn't stop anybody weighing in with their two cents. Not for a minute. Not a bit of it. Not on your fucking nelly! Worse than that, it didn't seem to occur to anybody that they were mind-farting. OK, people do it all the time – immigration, renationalisation, austerity… if we needed to see the research before we opened our mouths then all conversation would consist of a discussion on the weather. Then again, there's Wittgenstein: 'Whereof one cannot speak, thereof one must be silent'. And then again, these are educators, not a bunch of people hanging off the end of a bar.

I also know that if the Principal calls a meeting to discuss her decision, no one will come armed to that meeting with any consideration of the research. They won't prep. They'll just turn up. And talk. And talk some more, because there are no facts in their head getting in the way of the shit they're talking. Hell, if the 45th President of the United States can get away with it…

Strong stuff, what? Thing is, though, I'm not dumping on teachers. Really, I'm not. These are my colleagues and, for the most part, I admire them for the tough job they do (the *toughest*, remember). What I am giving out about is the mindset they have adopted or been forced to adopt. They are encouraged to see their job as just a job: to clock in day after day, nine to five, and simply teach. They aren't encouraged to think about their roles as educators, to keep abreast of new developments or new thinking in their discipline, or education in general. Instead, they pack their ham sandwiches into their lunchboxes, or scrape the remains of last night's yummy feast of lentils and beans into a Tupperware box, and come into school and just get on with it. Sure, we get notifications of courses being advertised, webinars that might prove useful, but it's totally ad hoc. It's the magpie approach to education, picking up bits and pieces here and there rather than any rigorous, systematic, serious idea of training. It's ironic that many of these courses will include a quote or a video segment from Ken Robinson. Robinson is the go-to guy. He is Mr Cool when it comes to education. One of his TED Talks is the most watched on YouTube. He says things like, 'Just because someone is in a classroom doesn't mean they are learning, just as someone being on a diet doesn't mean they are losing any weight.' Confucius say, wha? Yet he does have a point, and one of his main criticisms is that there isn't enough high-quality teacher training and development going on.

Look at Scandinavia, where teachers are regarded as academics, for Christ's sakes! Teaching enjoys a status and a respect akin to being a doctor, a lawyer or a scientist in those Nordic countries which regularly come top in global education league tables. Tellingly, they aren't paid that much better than British or Irish teachers. But look at the retention rates for teachers in Finland, for instance – 90 per cent. Why do they stay on there while young teachers here are fleeing for the gates and a job in a call centre? Basically, if you break it right down, I think it's because those Nordies think teaching is sort of like, well, a very important job, and those doing the job should feel valued and fulfilled in their work; that the people working with the next generation, the future of the country – the people filling kids' heads with ideas and values and making them as numerate and literate as possible – that these people should be happy, and more motivated as a result. Isn't that ridiculous? Isn't that just plain daft? No, hats off to those feisty Finns and those salty Swedish seadogs, for you can bet that if Erik or Elsa or Olaf or Krista weren't being treated as professionals, they wouldn't be hanging around, they'd be off with their skates over their shoulders, shooting moose and picking cloudberries.

But to do all this – to boost the professional standing of teachers, to improve their working environment, to enhance job satisfaction – all of this requires investment; it means time and resources. *It means money!*

Let's return to this 'mixed-ability' change the Principal is contemplating. Will there be adequate training for such a seismic shift in the way staff should plan their classes? What would you envisage – a series of day-long seminars over a period of a couple of months? At the least, all directed time after school until the end of the year to be devoted to such a radical new approach? Remember, most teachers will have taught 'set' classes since they left college. So what will be the plan? A pound to a penny, it involves someone from the Department for Education – they of 'Putting Care into Education' – coming in for an hour or two to tell us how to differentiate our lessons. And that will be it.

I'm serious... *that will be fucking it!*

I shit you not. Once again, done on the cheap. And we all know what happens to stuff that's done on the cheap, whether it be some plumbing that eventually floods your kitchen or that shiny black tarmacking on your drive that the fella with a Traveller brogue swears by as he jumps into his truck and gets the hell away before it starts to rain.

But you can't turn children into the entrepreneurs and the artists and, God forbid, the leaders of tomorrow on the cheap. It can't be done. Not if you don't want the country to be... well, cheap. And cheap as in a bit of tat, not cheap as in a bargain. In 2016, China committed $30 billion to education technology research over a four-year period. What did Britain commit? £1 million – *over three years!* What are they going to buy with that? Sweetie lollipops, after getting a good deal from You Sweetie, to be distributed amongst schools, maybe five to each school, so a few lucky kids can have something to suck on while they wait the twenty minutes or so for their computers to boot up?

For a graphic demonstration of the state of British schools, take the following example of a school who sent out an email to parents titled 'We Did the Maths...' followed by a photo of Post-its covered in rudimentary sums and the following message:

Dear Friends of St Elizabeth,

Our computers are broken and they take ages to come on! We really need some new laptops to use in class. We've done some maths. If each parent was to donate £5 and pass this donation link to four more friends we will raise enough to buy thirty new laptops.

Ah, bless their little cotton socks, eh? Every time you hear the latest Tory statistic/lie about more being pumped into education than ever before, remember the above. Increasingly, crowd-funding, Amazon wish lists and sponsored events are becoming a vital part of schools' efforts to close funding gaps. Meanwhile, Middle Eastern countries are pouring money into their schools and sucking in British-trained teachers at a rate of knots. Judging by the state of our schools, the only things they are attracting are rats (and I mean rats as in rodents, not rats as in the inspectorate; though there's a fair few of those creatures sniffing about too).

Is it any wonder our teachers react to any new initiative like someone's waving a rotten fish under their nose? Why should they give a damn when they are treated with so little respect, when they are constantly told to just bog on regardless?

Christ, you'd think they were professionals.

# 21 FEBRUARY

Mid-term!

I'm carrying a cold but I don't give a damn; it's mid-term. First item on the agenda: the pub. I order a taxi. David picks me up. David was in my first form-class. One of the things about teaching in a town where you live, you can't get away from it. If I roll out of this pub later on tonight, which, of course, I won't – I always obey the instruction on the bottle to 'drink responsibly' (I mean, what the fuck does that mean?) – but if I do, you can be sure I will run into a pupil or two. There have been times when I have tried to engage them in conversation just to prove I was not three sheets to the wind. That's never a good idea. Then again, teaching in a town where you live is generally not a good idea. You just can't get away from the fact that you are a teacher. It follows you around like a bad smell. Pop down to the shop for a paper and there's three pupils hanging around the front door. Odds are, one of them will be smoking. You've a decision to make: do you tell him or her to put the fag out, and risk a confrontation, or do you feign temporary blindness, which fools no one and lessens you in their eyes, and just walk on by? Of course, the thing is, you don't give a damn if they're smoking. You're just getting your paper. It's got nothing to do with you. But they think it has something to do with you. But then if you do tell them to put the fag out – if you do make it something to do with you – they will then tell you that it has fuck all to do with you. Work that out! Then there's the times you're dandering through the car park in Tesco, pushing your trolley, cursing the price of things these days, when suddenly a shout of 'Hey, cunt-face!' rolls across the car park like thunder. Everyone's looking at each other – old ladies, paraplegics, pregnant women, toddlers – asking themselves who this cunt-face could possibly be. But you know it's you and you must now feign temporary deafness again, and just get the hell out of there, because there's absolutely no winning in that situation.

Saying that, 'cunt-face' is just a general term of abuse, not a nickname. I know of one teacher who would regularly be assailed with cries of 'Fat-Cock' while he was just going about his business in the town. That was his nickname. For a long time, I was too polite to ask colleagues how he came by it. I was thinking the worst: that he'd flashed said large phallus at some kids or something. But, no, they called him Fat-Cock because he looked like one; I mean the general shape of him, over-large with his torso tapering off towards a neckless head which sat on his body like the helmet of a… well, fat cock. The base devilment of that nickname amazed me. And it terrified me too. This was how cruel children could be. I mean, this was a father, this was a husband; his own children would one day learn that their beloved dad was otherwise known as Fat-Cock. And, of course, I could never look at him in the same way again.

Yet confrontations and abuse, outside school hours, are not the norm. There's only a few head-bangers who will indulge in that. Generally, it's just that you can never shake off being a teacher. You walk down a street and you pass pupils nudging one another and going, 'There's yer man!' You go for a meal and find yourself seated by an ex-pupil who wants to talk about his schooldays. It's all very friendly, but basically you don't want to talk about his fucking schooldays, you want to enjoy your meal without interruption. Same with the pub (I don't want to bring up the pub again – I don't spend all my time in there): you're having a drink and here we go again with some blast from the past who wants a ramble down memory lane with his old teach. And if you don't want to go for that little walk down the highways and byways of their less-than-perfect recall – the guys who bother you in the pub were often prize shits in their time at school – they can sometimes cut up rough with a few drinks in them. Or, conversely, they may hold up their hands and tell you they completely understand, that they are sorry for being a nuisance. And that makes you feel like shit. It's a lose–lose.

But it's like being a minor celebrity. Or, in many instances, a demi-god. Pupils will tell you where they saw you at the weekend: 'Saw you in Asda, doing your shopping, sir!' 'Saw you going down North Street, sir!' 'Saw you coming out of the cinema, sir!' All of this breathless, like it was a secret between me and them, like I had appeared to them – and only them – in human form.

I remember one occasion when I had a really bad flu. I was laid up for about three days. Finally, I made it out of bed. I still felt like shit but I needed something – anything! – to eat and drove to the nearest garage. I was wearing a pair of crumpled jeans, an old jacket and a monkey hat. I hadn't shaved either, of course. I looked just how I felt, like someone who should have been rooting about in the bins outside the garage rather than buying anything inside it. Then I ran into two girls I teach. Their expressions were a picture. My shop-soiled incarnation left them speechless. They couldn't have looked more shocked. Any idea that I was human, or that I was sick; of my existence beyond those four classroom walls... not a chance! A character in Tina Fey's *Mean Girls* put it best when describing coming across a teacher outside school as 'like seeing a dog walk on its hind legs'. In this variation, we are a visitor from another world, and yet the paradox is that once we re-enter that other world – the school – we're very much human, and fair game.

David, my taxi driver, perfectly exemplified this, and he's probably the reason it's all in my head. I'll always remember a question he asked me. 'Sir,' he said. 'Do you wear a suit and tie at home?' It was such a ridiculous question and yet he was perfectly serious.

Now, on the way to the pub, I ask him if he recalls asking me that.

'Can't remember that, sir.'

That's another thing. This man, who must be out of school twenty years, still calls me 'sir'. They all do. Even the prize shits in the pub. It's another facet of that paradox again – deep respect, reverence even, for the role, the position; yet often so little respect for the actual practice of the job.

'What age are you now, David?' I said, making conversation. 'Thirty-five?'

'What, sir? I'll be forty in October,' he says. 'Time flies, doesn't it, sir?'

Christ; suddenly I really needed that drink.

# 25 FEBRUARY

Thought long and hard. Not at school – God forbid. No, at home. Last night. That cold I was carrying at the start of mid-term turned into a full-blown chest infection. I was over it by the Saturday but that was mid-term gone for a Burton. I felt I was owed another week's holiday and was tempted to pull a sickie. As a colleague of mine once opined, 'Why would you pull a sickie when you were sick? Fuck that, pull it when you can enjoy it!' There were only two problems with that line of thinking, neither of them to do with any feelings of duty or responsibility. (Those go out the window when you lose almost every free period you get. I've calculated I've worked at least an extra two weeks of teaching time with the amount of periods I've covered so far this year.) No, nothing to do with those arcane concepts. Rather, the first problem was that the Principal herself expects a phone call first thing if you're going to be off sick. It used to be a designated teacher taking the call but now she's made herself the designated teacher. Crafty, that. Same with the back-to-school interview system she's initiated. It isn't peculiar to our school – most schools are doing it now – but the old regime didn't care for it. It's all supposed to be a pastoral consideration. God forbid a teacher should return to school after an illness without a word of sympathy from the Principal. Bollix, if you ask me! The whole idea of it is to make a teacher think twice about whether to ring in or not.

And it works.

I don't ring in. I go into school. First thing, I look at the cover rota on the noticeboard in the concourse and whaddya know – I've lost my only free! Some other bastard didn't think twice. I could curse my sense of duty and responsibility, but, as I said, they didn't come into it. Instead, I curse my cowardice and any child who's going to have the nerve to cross me this day.

9C slouch into my room trailing that black cloud that seems to hang perpetually over them. I'm not joking. It's a spring day outside but the atmosphere seems to darken; shadows swirl in the corners of the room like smoke. I'm in no mood for them. We're starting a new unit of work, 'The Language of Persuasion': analysing charity leaflets, advertisements, famous speeches. Did I say my day couldn't get any worse? It's only ten past nine and I can only hope this day will be thoroughly forgettable rather than actively unpleasant.

How did I plan to start this unit? I scribbled something down in my planner before mid-term. 'Scribbled' is the word. I can hardly read my own writing. Something about the sale of 'erotic pets'? What the fuck? Oh, *exotic* pets. Now

I remember. We look at a photocopy of an RSPCA leaflet highlighting the dangerous trade in animals like snakes, lizards and turtles. I talk about the purpose of the document, its audience, the use of headlines, typeface, bullet points, emotional language, passive and active verbs...

I'm boring the tits off myself!

Then there's 9C. There's just no spark with them. They're just one of those classes who seem to lack any real personality. Nice kids, decent work... but no fire. Today of all days, that's not good enough. My plan had been to run through a checklist of terms with which to analyse a document such as the RSPCA leaflet; provide them with a framework by which they could forensically interrogate it. But fuck it. I just tell them to give me a page on it. Next lesson, they'll read out the garbage they've written, and we can talk about why it's garbage, and then we can get on with how to plan a proper response. Next lesson. Not today. Don't put off until tomorrow what you can do today... *my backside!* The Russian novelist Ivan Turgenev wrote: 'The word tomorrow was invented for indecisive people and small children.' And teachers. Turgenev forgot teachers who were on the point of spontaneous combustion.

After 9C it was 10B. Mercifully, half of them were missing because of a netball match. I had planned to run through their assessments, but there was little point with so many absent. Instead I dusted off my old grammar book and set them an exercise on synonyms and antonyms.

With fifteen minutes to go we began to correct it. Shamus

had to write a sentence with an antonym of 'cheap'. He wrote this: 'Mr Brown's Zygomatic Arch repairal surgery cost an extortionate amount because of the fact that he lived in America.'

Obviously, Obamacare didn't cover it. Where Shamus plucked this from, I have no idea. But it's pretty good for a shitty little exercise from my grammar book to cover a dead period.

A few answers later, it was Conor's turn. Conor had to write a sentence with an antonym of 'smooth'. 'The stone was rough,' says he, and flops back in his seat, exhausted.

Any another time I might have just sighed and moved on. Not today, Satan. I asked Conor if he wanted a towel to mop his brow after pushing that huge boulder up the hill of his imagination. Maybe he needed a pillow and a wee lie down after such a Herculean effort? He smiled. I smiled. My voice was dangerously soft and reasonable, little more than a hiss. 'Fourteen years on the planet and that's the best you can do when asked to find an antonym of "smooth" and write a sentence?'

Conor shrugged.

Wrong thing to do.

I exploded. 'Fourteen bloody years and that's the limit of your vocabulary!'

The upshot was that Conor was set the entire exercise again. 'And if you so much as come close to "the stone was rough", you'll do it again. And again, and again. Until I'm satisfied!' I pointed at Shamus. 'Shamus, read me out your sentence for an antonym of "smooth". Shamus gulped. He has this thing where he twirls his pen like it's a drumstick. It's a nervous tic. The pen was a blur between his fingers. 'Rough, surging waves lashed against the galleon and it lurched on the storm-tossed sea as it rounded the treacherous Cape of Good Hope.'

'You hear that?' I sounded like I was the mad captain of that ship, roaring in the face of that storm: a frothing, fuming, spuming Ahab cursing the vagaries of Fate and its decision to give me this life, rather than one where I could live off an inheritance and wouldn't need 'sick' days. 'You hear that? I want galleons, I want storm-tossed seas, I want the treacherous Cape of Good bloody Hope. *Do you get me, Conor?*'

To return to the vexed question of mixed ability I considered a few entries earlier, I suppose it all depends on your approach.

Lunch was a union meeting. It was too depressing for words. Basically, we were fucked; if not by the pupils, then by the Education Authority. I had nothing useful to contribute and neither did anyone else, though of course it didn't stop them talking. (It seems that none of my colleagues have read any Mark Twain: 'It is better to keep your mouth shut and appear stupid than to open it and remove all doubt.') After lunch, it was the lost free. The absentee was a PE teacher. I've never liked PE teachers. Grown men and women who aren't drug-dealers (at least, I don't think they are) wearing tracksuits to work!

10P was last period. They're usually bouncing at the end of the day but today they were tolerable. Maybe they caught my mood.

After the bell, walking to my car, for the thousandth, thousandth time those devastating questions of Wilfred Owen's ran through my head, 'Was it for this the clay grew tall? / —O what made fatuous sunbeams toil / To break earth's sleep at all?' Most people attribute these to Owen's experiences in the war. They forget that he was a teacher as well. It's my theory he wrote these particular lines prior to his enlistment: that in the classroom he learned all there was to be learned about man's inhumanity to man, long before he ever saw a trench or heard the whine of a mortar shell or strapped on a gas mask.

I think I should have made that call this morning.

# 28 FEBRUARY

This morning, Haley wrote this:

> Robert Swindells wrote stone cold. Stone cold was published in 1993. In stone cold there are two main characters, that are named Shelter and Link. In this novel, Shelter is the bad guy. Shelter pertends to be helpful to the homeless by giving them a home for the night. While Link is homeless who left school early and has no friends. The opening chapters introduce us to Link and Shelter. Shelter and Link wright this novel as two narrators. No this change of narration will not be a battle between these two characters. The change makes you want to read on.

This is to be the introduction to an essay on the novel. The title of the essay is: 'What makes the opening of *Stone Cold* interesting and engaging?' It's a Writer's Craft question, where the pupils are to analyse the methods employed by the writer to tell the story. Rather than just letting them get on with it, we will have a general discussion on the opening and then I'll provide them with a framework with which to structure the essay. The framework is a series of questions. If pupils answer these questions in full sentences, one after the other, and then run these sentences together with some basic linking phrases, they should have a decent essay.

The framework for the introduction was as follows:

1. Who wrote *Stone Cold* and in what year was it published?
2. Give a short summary of what happens in the novel.
3. Who do the opening chapters introduce us to?
4. How does the point of view change every chapter and is this unusual?
5. Does this change of point of view/narration suggest that the novel will be a battle between these two characters?
6. Does this make us want to read on?

All standard stuff. The point of view question (4) refers to the fact that the homeless man, Link, and the serial killer, Shelter, narrate alternate chapters for the length of the novel until the bloody conclusion when they finally meet face-to-face.

Cathal wrote this:

Robert Swindells wrote the Stone Cold book in 1993. Shelter tricked homeless people in to his house to his decieive and killed them. The opening introduces ous to the first character Shelter and how he got the name and how Link became. The change view changes evry tim. In one chatper Link is the narrater, then Shelter is the narrader this is unusual and yes this makes the reader want to read on to find out what heappens in the end.

Before I comment on Haley and Cathal's responses to the essay, I'd first like to state that these are two lovely kids. They're never in trouble and they are always well-mannered. They're the kind of kids you send with messages around the school because you know you can trust them absolutely. As my granny used to say, 'You could be dying about them!' i.e. they're great children.

And these great children will walk out of this school in two and half years' time with no qualifications worth talking about.

I taught them in first year. I didn't teach them last year. Now I'm teaching them again. What am I teaching them? That's a good question. Remember, though, they had seven years in primary school, and maybe a year in nursery before that, and the above is the best they can do. Ten or eleven years of education and this is the best they can do.

How the hell does that happen?

And what can I do about it? I know that whatever methods I employ, whatever teacher strategies I use, the above is not going to improve – not in its fundamentals, its basic illiteracy. In a class of sixteen other pupils, I have tried to give them as much one-on-one as I possibly could, both in first year and this year. I have sat down with Cathal time out of number and asked him to read through what he has written.

He sees where the mistakes are. He sees where he hasn't used a full stop. He sees where words are missing and where he has left a sentence dangling in mid-air. So he corrects these mistakes to the point where he has written something close to what he means in his head. Yet the next time he is set an exercise, he makes all the same mistakes again. I mean the *exact* same mistakes. Then we go through the same rigmarole. It's the same with Haley.

Ever decreasing circles. Circles of Hell, when you consider this is only the introduction to their essays. Next week we get to do it all again with their first paragraph. The following week will be their second paragraph. The final week will be their conclusion. That's four weeks of me butting my head against a wall and Cathal and Haley nodding hopelessly at my corrections.

For what?

I've corrected both of their introductory pieces, going through the text word by word with them both. Haley's now reads:

Robert Swindells wrote Stone Cold. It was published in 1993. In Stone Cold there are two main characters, Shelter and Link. In this novel, Shelter is the bad guy and he pretends to be helpful to the homeless by giving them a bed for the night. But he kills them. Link is homeless; he left school early and had trouble at home. The opening chapters introduce us to Link and Shelter. Shelter and Link write the novel as two narrators. This change of narration

suggests the novel will be a battle between these two characters. Looking forward to this battle between a young
homeless person and a vicious killer of homeless people
makes us eager to read on to see what will happen.

Cathal's reads:

Robert Swindells wrote Stone Cold in 1993. The novel is
about homelessness. Shelter, a serial killer, tricks homeless
people into his house. He deceives them and kills them.
The opening introduces us to the first character, Shelter,
and how he got his name and how Link got his name. The
point of view changes all the time. In one chapter Link
is the narrator and then Shelter is the narrator in the
next chapter. This is unusual and makes the reader want
to read on to find out what happens in the end between
these two characters.

I believe these are close to what Haley and Cathal wanted to
say.

The thing is, though, that they will never say what they
want to say first time round. Not without serious expert
intervention; not without serious expert help. As I've said
before, I'm not an expert on SEN kids. Even if I was, I can't
provide the care and attention needed in a class with up to
twenty other pupils, many of them with their own problems,
and the way things are going, those class numbers are only
going to rise.

But what costs less? Helping these children now, so that they might leave school with some level of literacy and numeracy that might prove the springboard to a life where they are able to fend for themselves and make some contribution to society, or not helping them and committing to more state intervention down the line in the form of welfare and healthcare (and possibly the hand of the justice system), the result of a life of subsistence?

I know the right response to that and so do you.

# 1 MARCH

Ah, the end of February!

We're not in the clear yet, not by a long stick of chalk that's lying in the back of a drawer somewhere and will never be used again in this age of progress, but we're getting there. I have a theory which I think should be up there with Einstein's thoughts on relativity. I think time passes much faster when you are a teacher, that more than any other profession, we live our lives in cycles, each year a lung-busting push toward the heady days of July. We live our lives wishing much of it away.

I should write a paper on it. Like Einstein, who never even made the shortlist when he applied to be a teacher of General Science at a secondary school in Berne, even though he included his paper on the Theory of Relativity in his submission for the position (proof, if proof were needed, that Boards of Governors don't know shit!). I'll bet though that if he had become a teacher and then found fame and fortune, you wouldn't have seen old Albert for spacedust: no, he wouldn't have been demonstrating some of his musings on the speed of light, that simply would have been the velocity with which he was exiting that school building. Yet reminiscing about his teaching experience years later, he would have talked about it in glowing terms and probably mentioned how much he enjoyed the energy and curiosity of the kids. That seems to be the general consensus with ex-teachers who have prospered in other fields. Out like a shot they were, never to butter another ham sandwich. But when interviewed on a book tour or while promoting their new film and asked about those early years, they will smile warmly and rhapsodise about their memories of being cloistered for hours on end in the fetid atmosphere of a classroom filled with postpubescents.

Ho-hum…

A writer came in to do a talk last year. He was about the same age as me. I got speaking to him. He said he used to be a teacher. Said he loved it. 'Why did you quit?' I asked him, a smile on my chops you couldn't have removed with a hammer. 'It wasn't feasible,' he said. 'Not with the writing.' Credit to the man, he even seemed to believe this himself. There he was, getting all excited: 'I love getting back to the classroom. I love the curiosity of children; the way they make you see the world in a new way – a better way.' I'm not joking, this dick actually talked like this. He rhapsodised about the wonder and innocence and delight of schoolchildren. I should have introduced him to Corey.

In the gym, in front of Year 8, he read a chapter from one of his novels before lapsing into that inspirational *X Factor* back-of-a-matchbox dreams-can-come-true Disney wisdom that is the common currency of those who have escaped the fray. This guy, this sage, talked about this whole idea of 'imagination', that some people think they have it and some people think they don't. He said that he thought that was all rubbish. He said that what we all had were memories and feelings, and story-telling was trying to turn these into something and believing that what was in our hearts and heads would be interesting to other people. If I caught the logic of it all correctly, this man was arguing that you didn't need ideas or any creative sensibility to write a story, instead all you needed was a pulse. The first years lapped this up like it was full cream. But if you pursued his logic a little further, there was no reason why dogs and cats shouldn't be flexing their literary paws and making the *New York Times* bestseller list or getting nominated for the Booker.

I endured a directed day a few years back where an 'in-spirational' speaker came in to give a talk to staff. On the walls of the room he had tacked up famous quotes. So there was Gandhi, 'Be the change you want to see in the world'; FDR, 'To handle yourself, use your head; to handle others, use your heart'; Sun Tzu, 'In the midst of chaos, there is also opportunity'; Simon Cowell, 'Even if the plate is broken, step up to it'; and so on, and so forth. Anyway, the first thing we were told to do was go and stand by a quote that we identified with. I stood vaguely next to Bob Marley's 'Some people feel the rain; others just get wet', not because I identified with it but because it was closest to where I was sitting. Of course, this being sod's law, the guy picks me out of a room full of other people to ask why I was standing there. I was struck dumb for about ten seconds before he asked me his second penetrating question: what did I think Marley meant by the statement? I wanted to laugh. No harm to the man, but as with much else of what he said or sang, Marley had probably been off his tits when he came up with this pearl of wisdom. In less robust language, I made this point. 'So why are you standing beside it?' asked my interlocutor. I didn't want to be rude. As I've said before, I hate rudeness. I wanted to say to this man that, in an age of Brexit and Trump and easy answers, I objected to this puerile nonsense and as far as I was concerned, he could take his aphorisms and stick them up his hole. But instead of saying that, I just shrugged and sighed and suggested a certain laziness of mind.

But back to our visiting writer. There was a report in the local paper about his visit. I'm in one of the photographs looking slightly startled, like I've just followed through. There were lots of comments from the kids saying how thrilled they were to meet a real-life writer, someone who 'made his living with words'. The writer himself is quoted as saying that every time he talks to schoolchildren he is 'inspired with a new hope'.

Yeah, me too.

# 4 MARCH

'As with the rainbow, a spectrum is a condition that is not limited to a specific set of values but can vary across a continuum, and therefore a spectrum symbolises change.'

I've re-read this I don't know how many times, and I haven't a fucking baldy what it means.

There was a special assembly this morning to announce the formation of 'Spectrum'. Pupils were told that this is for LGBTQ pupils and there will be a gathering every Wednesday afternoon at lunchtime for those who want to come along. In tandem with this, staff and pupils were also informed that one of the bathrooms, formerly a disabled bathroom, is now an all-gender bathroom. Or maybe it's still a disabled bathroom, as well as an all-gender bathroom, and no one mentioned that because it wouldn't have sounded quite right. Oh fuck, I don't know! These days, the whole question of sexuality leaves me horribly confused and I stay well away. As I say, I've read and re-read that definition of Spectrum, the definition that appears on the poster that is now displayed in my room – am I hip or what? – and

I still don't know what it means. Does sexuality change constantly? Is it fluid? I asked the teacher who had set up 'Spectrum' what it meant, and she merely repeated what it said on the poster and nodded sagely at me, so I nodded sagely back. Presumably this teacher is gay, lesbian, trans, bi, queer... what? I'm afraid to ask. I've been told a new word is 'questioning'.

I'm questioning, too, except I don't think it's the same line of questioning. But I remember my own school days and a 'questioning' friend of mine who made himself an ABBA badge. He wore it to school, this yellow badge as big as one of those giant swirl candy lollies, with ABBA written on it in blue felt-tip. Thinking back, a twelve-year-old walking down a busy school corridor with this monstrosity stuck to the pocket of his blazer like a sunflower... it was probably one of the bravest things I've ever witnessed, because he might as well have written on it, 'I AM GAY, KICK MY FUCK IN!' And, sure enough, that's exactly what happened. Thing is, he refused to stop wearing it. There'll be no books written about him; he won't go down as one of the heroes of the gay rights movement, but he wouldn't take off that badge no matter how many looterings he took. And when the badge was removed by force, he made himself a new one. You ask me, that's up there with Rosa Parks refusing to give up her seat. And the school authorities, did they support him in this campaign for self-determination? Ha! In a cunning manoeuvre, the Headmaster banned the wearing of all badges. But this boy was undaunted. He came to school the day after the ban with *two* ABBA badges stuck to his blazer like huge Swedish tits. For that, he got suspended. After that, the protest ended. Maybe he felt he'd made his point. Maybe his parents had kicked his fuck in. But, as I say, there'll be no songs written about that guy or statues erected in his honour.

How things have changed. For the better, of course. Of course, it's for the better. And yet... 'Spectrum' was the talk of the school. Judging from what I heard in my classes today, this new society – is that the right word? – is going to be inundated.

By children who are confused about their sexuality?

Or by children who are just confused?

Or who want to be confused?

Or cool?

Except what's 'cool' when it's at home?

A recent YouGov poll asked people to place themselves on a sliding scale where zero equals exclusively straight and six equals exclusively gay. More than a quarter of Britons identified as something other than 100 per cent heterosexual. Strikingly, amongst the eighteen to twenty-four age group, this statistic leapt to 49 per cent. What does this mean? Is it a cause for celebration? It could be argued that these are the most sexually liberated group of adults in British history. However – and I've touched on this before – it doesn't square with the fact that the number of teenage girls self-harming over the past ten years has doubled, or that the mental health charity stem4 found an 'epidemic' of anxiety, depression and suicidal thoughts amongst British school-children in its 2018 report. How does it tally with a survey conducted by the National Education Union of 8,600 school leaders, teachers and support workers where 83 per cent said they had witnessed an increase in the number of children in their care with poor mental health, rising to 90 per cent amongst students in colleges?

Sexual liberation?

Or sexual oppression?

With teenage girls, for instance, call me old-fashioned but I find it hard to reconcile liberation with their fixation with wearing clothes that, thirty years ago, a prostitute wouldn't have slipped into for fear of literally giving the game away. Chinese parents used to bind the feet of their daughters to make them more appealing to a suitor; take a look at our daughters of the West on a Friday or Saturday night tottering on outrageous heels, clinging to one another as if crossing a frozen lake. They don't need patriarchy to bind their feet; they do it to themselves. 'Power' heels! But where does the power lie? When asked what was so attractive about women in high heels, the French shoe designer Christian Loubou-tin replied that it was that the heels slowed a woman down, giving the man more time to look at her. Trapped in the male gaze or what? You may have escaped the kitchen, ladies, but you're not going anywhere in a hurry. I hate to bang on, but these are shoes that give our erstwhile Boadiceas hammer toes, bunions, Morton's neuroma, metatarsalgia, Haglund's deformity, osteoarthritis, tendonitis, sciatica, back pain, degenerative joint disease, shortened calf muscles, an altered gait and a very much increased chance of breaking their bloody ankles. But, hey, it's not just footwear. There's some much bigger con going on here; all those girl bands, those role-models, prancing on stage with their knickers showing, wearing basques and thigh-high rubber boots; all those fem-dom Aphrodites who proclaim their femininity while flashing their tits... and, as ever, the fellas in the back row are smiling like apes and wanking themselves into a coma. Are they powerless in the face of these goddesses or are they just having the best time they could possibly imagine? I remember watching a news segment about *Forbes* categorising Jennifer Lopez as one of the world's most powerful women. Without so much as a dash of irony, the segment cut from a sober-sided executive lauding Lopez's hard-headed business acumen to a posed photograph of Jenny from the Block looking all lovely in a corset and a pair of lace-up boots, an outfit that Frank-N-Furter from *Rocky Horror* would've have blushed at. Nobody seemed to see anything wrong with this picture – one of the world's most powerful women dressed up like an extra from *Debbie Does Dallas*. OK, that's part of the package with J-Lo, same as Beyoncé; theirs is an Amazonian perfection, an otherness and beauty which almost transcends sex. But what are these powerful and no doubt very intelligent women saying to the young girls who worship them? Whatever that message is, I think it's getting lost in translation. To me, liberation is kicking against the pricks – my old classmate with the ABBA badge – not adopting an ironic, knowing, coy bunny-girl pose in front of them. I don't see sexual liberation; I see a strangled, witless conformity. I see the unquestioning mentality of the herd. I see what's-hot and what's-not.

And I think Spectrum is in the same ballpark.

Though I'm not going to say that out loud. I don't want to be condemned as a questioning-basher.

# 5 MARCH

Just in from the Education Training Inspectorate. It seems they haven't been able to complete inspection reports on 161 schools in the past year. Ah, the poor dears! Then this from a spokeswoman:

> It is regrettable that due to action by the teaching unions, some schools have not been co-operating with the ETI. Our focus is on ensuring that all learners are getting a good education. This protracted period of action... prevents ETI from highlighting where improvements are needed and in some cases urgent improvements are needed. A failure to implement these improvements may ultimately have a detrimental impact on the learner.

All very reasonable, wouldn't you say?

Then put it beside this from Julian Stanley, CEO of the Education Support Partnership:

> In 2017–18, we managed over 8,600 cases through our

helpline and worked directly with over 600 educational establishments to help them put in place programmes to encourage staff wellbeing. This represents a 35 per cent increase in teachers using our helpline compared to last year. We also saw a 42 per cent increase in financial grant applications – the demand for our services has never been higher.

What is the Education Support Partnership? It's a charity organisation for teachers. That's right – a charity for teachers. Admittedly it's been around for a while, over 140 years, but it's never been so busy as it is now. In 2017 it conducted a comprehensive health survey and found that 75 per cent of teaching staff had faced physical or mental health issues in the previous two years because of their work. I'll give you that astonishing statistic again because I think it needs repeating – *seventy-five per cent!*

You got that?

The ECP's report also makes clear that much of this mental and physical distress is because of financial hardship. Stanley continues: 'We have seen a significant increase in the number of teachers facing homelessness, which is particularly noticeable in the south and south-east [of England]. We're awarding more grants than we have ever awarded in our history. The applications we receive can be terribly distressing.' To go back to the ETI and their regret at the action of the teaching unions, the unions had advised non-co-operation with the ETI because of a pay offer that would see staff receive no across-the-board pay rise for 2015/16 and a 1 per cent cost of living uplift for 2016/17. This after the public sector pay freeze of the previous five years. Insulting doesn't even come close!

The ETI's report speaks of the 'detrimental impact on the learner'.

But of the detrimental impact on the teacher?

You guessed it – not a dickybird.

Homelessness amongst teachers. That's a doozy, isn't it? Those aren't words that are supposed to be in the same sentence. Makes you think of all those other people out there scraping by and clinging on by the very fingernails in supposedly less secure employment. A study by the Resolution Foundation think tank estimates the proportion of children in Britain living in poverty will hit a record high of 37 per cent by 2023/24 as incomes stagnate and benefit cuts continue to bite. *Thirty-seven per cent!* I keep italicising these statistics and repeating them but, I mean, this is the land of Shakespeare and Milton, of Blake, of Newton, of Hawking, of the Beatles and Bowie, and in that land more than one in three children are going to be living in poverty! How's that for a detrimental impact on learners?

Anybody still think the ETI's looking through the right end of the telescope?

Not a word from them about teachers' welfare. Hey, how about schools themselves and their situation? The head-teachers' campaigning group WorthLess? has calculated that school budgets have been reduced in real terms by 8 per cent per pupil since 2010. Many schools are considering moving to a four-and-a-half-day week to save money. In a 2019 *Observer* article, Cambridge primary school head Tony Davies lambasted the government's

> astonishingly myopic vision for the future of this country. People talk about knife crime. That is just a symptom of a far deeper, wider malaise, which is that we are draining the potential and the hope of young people by cutting their services, labelling their schools as failing and labelling them, as individuals, as failures. It has a cumulative, devastating impact, and what else can you expect but for young people to feel angry, disaffected and isolated?

Consider the 2018 report of the United Nations Special Rapporteur, Professor Philip Alston, and his assessment of poverty and human rights in the UK, the world's fifth largest economy. I mean, this is the guy who gets sent to places like Haiti and sub-Saharan Africa. Here he was popping his head up in darkest Belfast and Glasgow and Newcastle and the like, where he reported that fourteen million people, a fifth of the population, live in poverty, with four million of these more than 50 per cent below the poverty line, and 1.5 million destitute – *destitute!* – and unable to afford basic essentials. Alston concluded:

> British compassion for those who are suffering has been replaced by a punitive, mean-spirited, and often callous

approach apparently designed to instill discipline where it is least useful, to impose a rigid order on the lives of those least capable of coping with today's world, and elevating the goal of enforced blind compliance over a genuine concern to improve the well-being of those at the lowest levels of British society.

Anybody resigning in absolute shame over this?

Anybody in this excuse of a government even pretending to give so much as a flying fuck about this?

Consciously or not, Alston's conclusions echo the logic of the workhouse. More than 150 years ago, Dickens ridiculed the utilitarian men on the Poor Law boards who were 'very sage, deep, philosophical men' who had determined that the old poor law system failed to encourage the work ethic. In its place 'they established the rule that all poor people should have the alternative (for they would compel nobody, not they) of being starved by a gradual process in the house, or by a quick one out of it'. Inmates would receive:

> periodically small quantities of oatmeal; and ... three meals of thin gruel per day, with an onion twice a week, and half a roll on Sundays ... It was rather expensive at first, in consequence of the increase in the undertaker's bill, and the necessity of taking in the clothes of all the paupers, which fluttered loosely on their wasted, shrunken forms, after a week or two's gruel.

So, what's to be done? For a start, we could remember another celebrated Victorian radical, Shelley:

> Rise, like lions after slumber
> In unvanquishable number!
> Shake your chains to earth like dew
> Which in sleep had fallen on you
> Ye are many – they are few.

Yes, remember Shelley, or a more recent radical, Johnny Rotten: 'There is no future in England's dreaming'. Whichever way you want to play it, we all need to wake up and smell the dog shit and the damp and the despair. We need to stop meekly accepting this quite deliberate and calculated humiliation – in our schools, our hospitals, our public life – otherwise this ship is headed for the rocks. Iceberg. Whatever.

Mark my words.

In red pen.

# 7 MARCH

World Book Day.

'Bliss it was in that dawn to be alive. But to be young was very heaven!'

These were the words with which I greeted 10P. They looked at me askance. Generally, they're not used to such effusion on my part. When I say generally, I mean never. And the sources of such high spirits? World Book Day? Wise up! No, ten minutes earlier I had been informed that Freddy Fitness was in the building.

Wow! Yes! Yes, sir! Yabba dabba doo! Yippee-ki-yay, motherfucker!

Am I some health nut? That kind of person who hits fifty and realises their life will have been empty unless they've done the New York marathon? One of those poor benighted souls who holds their nose every morning and suppresses their gag reflex (and their sphincter) while they pour broccoli and kale smoothies down their throat? Not at all. Admittedly, I've got one of those fat-buster belts at home, and now and again I strap it to my belly and switch it on while

I lie back with a beer in one hand and a fag in the other. If anybody disturbs me and asks me what I'm doing, I tell them I'm working out.

So why such joy over Freddy Fitness? Now, I have no idea who Freddy Fitness is or even if he is a person. All I know is that he/they/it are doing something this morning... *and I'm free up until break!* I'll only have to look at 10P for a matter of minutes before they're whisked off to do press-ups or push-ups or some such other shite. And then I'm free. There's nothing like an unexpected free to put a spring in your step, to make your heart soar, to make you think the world really isn't such a bad place after all, and that the arc of the moral universe is indeed long, and does indeed bend towards justice, and soon enough all those Brexiteers are going to burn in hell.

But one should always remember the words of T. S. Eliot, and I think they are particularly applicable to teaching: 'Between the idea / And the reality / Between the motion / And the act / Falls the Shadow'. The shadow in this case being the PE teacher's as he stood at the door of my room, clipboard in hand. Did I tell you how much I hate PE teachers? 'Right there,' he says. 'Who's paid for Freddy Fitness, then?'

I did a double take. I jumped like my heart had been poked with a stick. All the colour drained from my face. Pay? Nobody said anything about paying.

Only two hands went up.

And the bottom fell out of my day.

When the PE teacher and these two pupils were gone, I

remonstrated miserably and at length with the rest of 10P. I told them I just didn't understand this younger generation. I didn't. I really didn't. Contrary to so much I say to them, I actually meant this. There was emotion in my voice. I had to clear my throat at least twice. I told them how very, very disappointed I was in them; that disappointed, even though twelve letters long, was too small a word. Did they care nothing for their physical health? Was it all just computers and Xboxes and bloody phones? Here's Freddy Fitness, the famous Freddy Fitness, the esteemed Freddy Fitness, the great Freddy Fitness, the sainted Freddy Fitness, coming to our school out of the goodness of his heart, to make sure their hearts were working properly... and what thanks did he get, the poor man, the poor ignorant soul? I shook my head at such ingratitude, at such... such...

Aw, fuck, now I had to teach them!

This black thought was marauding through my skull when Hannibal Lecter walked in. That is, 10P's classroom assistant was dressed as Hannibal the Cannibal for World Book Day. At first I thought this was a terrorist incident, confronted as I was by this woman wearing a boiler suit and a strange face mask. Then she told me she was going to eat my liver with some fava beans and a nice Chianti. At least, I reasoned that was what she said, since it was difficult to make her out behind the mask and she seemed to be having trouble breathing. I didn't know what use she, or most of the rest of the staff who were dressed up like dickheads, were going to be today. I don't go in for this stuff: this getting-down-with-the-kids shit, trying to convince them we're really human beings and can be quite fun people some of the time. Plus, I've always imagined the nightmare scenario during one of these 'fun' days, when someone like Corey has crossed way over the line and you're trying to discipline him and convince him of the seriousness of his offence; you're frothing at the mouth, spitting platitudes, while your wig's itching and your mascara's running and your huge plastic chest is cutting your nipples off because you've taken the manifestly wrong decision to come to school dressed as Dolly Parton or Jeremy Clarkson.

So, not for me. There was a European Day two years ago. The idea was that teachers dressed up as if they were from a foreign country. So you had someone coming in dressed like a matador, for instance. Then you had a French tart. At least, I think this teacher was a French tart. Either that or she had just dressed as normal and decided to grab a beret off the coat rack that morning as she dashed out to work. Then there was the teacher who came as a Roman centurion. This was decidedly ill-judged. Underneath the centurion skirt, the guy wore a pair of purple speedos. I can tell you this not because I lifted his skirt but because the uniform was for a much shorter person and everyone could see the speedos. Two helmets were visible: the one on his head and the one in his trunks. And he walked around like this all day, his cape flowing behind him, holding a sword in one hand and a shield in the other, with the flattened spheres of his bollocks on full display. In other circumstances, he would have been arrested.

I didn't dress up then either. I was the only one who didn't. What a rebel, eh? I was wearing a black suit. Then again, I'd been wearing it all week, and the week before if I remember rightly. So I told anyone who asked that I was Johnny Cash, sans guitar and a shroud, and hummed 'Ring of Fire' all day, this in reference not to Johnny and Americana but India and the hot curry I'd eaten the night before.

But back to the present. There was a new poster up beside the one for Spectrum in the concourse. I read it as Snow White and Cleopatra and SpongeBob SquarePants walked by. The poster was in the shape of a heart and it had an umbrella as the watermark. The title was 'Non-Binary' and underneath this it said, 'An umbrella term for a person who identifies or expresses a gender identity that is neither entirely male nor entirely female'. Beneath this there were speech bubbles with titles and explanations:

| ANDROGYNOUS | Identifying and/or presenting as neither specifically masculine nor feminine. |
|---|---|
| GENDER FLUID | One who expresses fluidity of gender identity. |
| AGENDER | One who does not identify as a particular gender. |
| GENDER NON-CONFORMIST | One whose physical or behavioural characteristics do not correspond to the traditional expectations of their gender. |
| GENDERQUEER | One who does not identify with a single fixed gender. |

Like the original Spectrum poster, I read and re-read this, and I did so out of a genuine desire to know what Spectrum means. So all these definitions mean the same thing, right?

Or wrong? If right, why have five names for them? If wrong, what's the difference? And Spectrum wasn't for people who defined themselves as gay or lesbian or bisexual or transgender, it was for people who refused to identify with any identification? Or is that bisexuality? Or is that queer as in questioning? Is this the Q in LGBTQ?

I'm not trying to be funny. This time, I'm really not. I do not understand this. I'm trying to, but I don't. All I know, or imagine, is that if I were thirteen or fourteen or fifteen and confused already – and not just about sexual identity – I'd be even more confused.

Like 8D.

Except their confusion is about sentences. I found out today that 8D don't know what a sentence is. We were doing an exercise on simple and compound sentences and conjunctions. It started off easy enough. I gave them two simple sentences and they were to join them together using 'and', 'but' or 'so', i.e. 'I put on my coat' / 'I went to the park' became 'I put on my coat *and* went to the park'. Straightforward. Primary school stuff. We were all having a great old time until I introduced the idea of clauses which begin with 'who' or 'which'. We were working from a textbook and looked at the sentence 'The bear fell into the bin.' I explained that clauses beginning with 'who' or 'which' can be added to the middle of a sentence in order to add information. For instance: 'The bear, who was scared of the dog, fell into the bin.' 8D nodded sagely. I gave them another sentence to which they were to add a clause beginning with 'who' or 'which'. The sentence was 'The cat licked its paws', except that I put it on the board as 'The cat _____ licked its paws', the space indicating where they should insert the clause (not claws) beginning with 'who' or 'which'. I was looking for something like, 'The cat, who had eaten its dinner, licked its paws', or 'The cat, which sat by the window, licked its paws'. Nothing too taxing. What did I get? The first hand up read her sentence: 'The cat who licked its paws.' I asked for a second response. This second response was the same as the first. So was the third. And so was the rest.

How did that happen?

How had the class so totally misunderstood my instruction?

Had I explained it badly? I don't think so. Maybe I hadn't given them enough examples beforehand? Really? This was straightforward stuff. Were they just being lazy? No, there are a lot of pupils in the class who are not lazy and they'd cocked this up.

No. No to all of the above. The only conclusion was that after seven years of schooling they did not know what a sentence was. Which would explain a lot: for instance, their inability to use a full stop properly. Every time I mark their work, the pages look measled with the red dots I've had to insert. So I began again, only this time, I tried to explain how 'The cat who licked his paws' was not a sentence. It might look like a sentence – it might have a noun and a verb, it might have a capital letter and a full stop – but it was not a sentence. Why? Because we're waiting on what the cat who licked its paws is going to do, or why it was licking its paws, or where it was when it was licking its paws etc., etc. Only then will it make a sentence. A sentence must make sense in and of itself. 'The cat who licked his paws' does not make sense in and of itself.

I tried again with another sentence. 'The book _____ was a very good read.' I asked for a response. The first response was 'The book which was a very good read.'

You can despair sometimes. Oftentimes. You can drop your head and ask yourself what the fuck you are doing here. You look out of the window and see another world: another life you might have had where you were doing something more useful, like emptying bins, or delivering pizzas, or handing out flyers, or stacking shelves, or being dressed up as a chicken with a sandwich board over your shoulders advertising fried chicken. Yeah, you can daydream about that other, more satisfying, fulfilling life...

Or you can try a little psychological warfare. There was half an hour left until dinner. I told 8D that if they really concentrated, and if they really listened to what I was saying, and if they were then able to give me a satisfactory answer to the next sentence, I would let them relax for the rest of the class. Not only that, but I'd let them go early for dinner and they'd make the top of the line. Then I laid it on even thicker and promised I would let them listen to music on their phones... *if they got the next sentence right.*

There wasn't a sound.

If I'd been standing there with a semi-automatic rifle, I couldn't have had any more of their attention.

I wrote 'The baby _____ sat in its buggy' on the board and repeated all that I'd repeated before.

Repetition, repetition, repetition: a teacher's mantra (that and 'July, July, July!').

After that, there was nothing but prayer.

Jenny puts up her hand. I nod at her. 'The baby...' she says. 'Yes?' I say, my voice strained with hope. 'The baby, who was crying, sat in its buggy.' After that, it was an avalanche. 'The baby, who had just had its nappy changed, sat in its buggy.' 'The baby, who was cute, sat in its buggy.' 'The baby, who was licking its ice cream, sat in its buggy.'

We had got there. Chalk one up for me. And them. After a solid hour of hard effort, 8D now knew what a sentence was. Hopefully, the next time I ask them, without the bribery of a hot dinner and ten minutes on their phones, they still know.

What's it like to be a teacher?

This is what it's like to be a teacher.

Now pay me!

# 12 MARCH

Took a sickie today. Phoned the Principal at seven o'clock this morning and told her I was in hospital. That chest infection never quite cleared up. I woke up in the middle of the night feeling like somebody had a pillow over my head.

Alanis Morissette would love it: the irony of thinking of taking a sickie two weeks back, and now here I am in Ward 3 North surrounded by seventy- and eighty-year-olds with respiratory problems. They all look like they're on the way out while I, too, am contemplating my own mortality. Am I old enough now that the cold of winter has become dangerous? Surely not.

But, as I say, here I am.

The last time I was in here was with my father. Then that nightmare began. I think about him all day as the doctors do their tests on me. I'm scared, afraid they'll find something... *sinister!* Isn't that the most frightening word in the English language? That and 'September'. Plus, there are needles. I fucking hate needles. I'd make the world's worst junkie. The thought of teaching the biggest head-bangers in the school last two on a Friday doesn't terrify me like needles terrify me. And these are those big needles where they actually tell you this is going to bloody hurt: 'You might feel some discomfort.' Jesus, I hate euphemisms almost as much as I hate needles.

As I say, I'm frightened, frightened the way my father was frightened when they did all those tests on him. I remember the consultant smiling thinly. 'Francis, we have a problem.'

Houston, we have a problem!

'You see that, Francis?' The consultant pointed to the scan – a cross-section of my father's shoulder and neck area. There was a mass of some sort on the back of my father's neck. The consultant called it a lesion and I thought of another Tom Hanks film, *Philadelphia*. That was what they called the running sores that started to appear on his body in the movie – lesions. And in the movie he had AIDS.

But this wasn't AIDS. AIDS is treatable these days.

My father had been unwell for a while. Since Christmas, really. A sociable man, he had stopped going to his local GAA club for a few drinks with his mates on a Friday night. On a Saturday night he would take my mother down to the same club. She was seventy-six and he was seventy-five but they still enjoyed these nights out, even if a few of their friends had fallen by the wayside. Now my mother and father were falling by that same wayside. My father just didn't feel up to it. More alarmingly, he had stopped going to the bookies. Now he just rang his bets through. A few years previously, he had been diagnosed with COPD and now he couldn't walk any kind of distance without having to stop and catch his breath. He was a smoker, at least a thirty-a-day man. Then at the beginning of April, just before Easter, he had begun to complain of a pain in his neck. Within a week, his right arm had gone numb. His GP diagnosed a slipped disc in his neck, recommended exercise and physiotherapy and packed him off with lots of codeine.

My father tried various physiotherapists and even acupuncture, all at £40 or so a touch for half-hour sessions, paid for by himself. They left him out of pocket and feeling worse. The day after these sessions he would be in agony. Then again, maybe he was being forced to use muscles he didn't normally use. Similarly, the weight he was losing – was that down to the fact that his medication was constipating him? Was that why he wasn't eating? And if he wasn't eating… As I've come to realise, when we're scared, we'll search high and low for the wrong answers. My father went back to his GP. This time, I went with him. The GP was reasonableness itself. He held out his hands, open and honest to all the world, and repeated his prognosis – a slipped disc. The reason? TMB: Too Many Birthdays. He recommended my father try to improve his posture and do some neck exercises *with a tennis ball!* I kid you not. He got sent home to find a tennis ball. I mean, I knew the NHS was in a bad way, but… Anyway, he was to place the tennis ball between the back of his neck and the backrest of his chair and rotate the ball between the two. Anybody who didn't know what he was doing would've thought he was having a stroke. Either that or that he was on the best drugs known to mankind. But they were to come later.

The pain intensified. I remember being shocked when he rang me one morning. He left a message on my answerphone. He had never mastered voicemail and always started talking before the beep so I only ever caught half of what he was saying. But what he was saying on this message didn't matter. It was his voice. It was so weak. It was a croak. Hearing it on the machine, my guts turned to ice. And I knew. I think from that moment I knew.

So did my mother. She had been our Cassandra, whispering dark warnings. She insisted on a second opinion. We went to A&E. I dropped my father and mother off at the hospital at 1 p.m. At 6 p.m., not having heard a word from them and having rung the house three or four times, I drove back over to the hospital. In a packed casualty department, I asked the receptionist where my father was. After five hours, he had just been shown through to one of the cubicles for examination. We waited another hour before a doctor examined him. This doctor concurred that the problem might well be a slipped disc but said that a scan was necessary. On the NHS, the scan might take up to two or three months. This was 23 May. My father died on 24 August. Work it out.

But my brother had private health insurance that came with his job. Someone once tried to sell me private health insurance and I told them in great detail exactly what I thought of their proposal and what they could do with it. Yeah, principles are great – but so is living. With great glee, my father would regularly point out the inconsistencies in my politics, like my concern for the environment. 'Aye,' he'd say, in his own inimitable way, 'Global warming! And there was you collecting for the miners back in the day. Didn't give two shits about the polar bear then!'

On 30 May I drove my father to the private clinic for the scan. I marvelled at the chandeliers, and the receptionists who looked and dressed and smiled like air hostesses. There was a list of consultants on the wall of the waiting room: I lost count at over a hundred. Our consultant said the scan would take twenty minutes. It took forty-five. I asked my father why it took so long. 'They put me in again,' he said. 'Oh fuck,' I thought. We were to come back the next week for the results.

That would be Tuesday 6 June.

That would be 'Francis, we have a problem.'

That would be the beginning of the end.

So we looked at that lesion, a white knotty swirl on the scan. Then my father looked at me and I looked at him. There was naked fear in his eyes and I suppose the same in mine. Some moments you never forget. The consultant explained that he was giving us a letter to bring to the Royal Victoria Hospital. He recommended that we made our way there immediately for further investigation. I asked why my father couldn't be treated at the clinic for... well, for whatever this was. The consultant said that only the NHS dealt with this, erm, level of complication.

*That word cancer is a real fucker!*

So, from the private clinic, we drove across Belfast to the Royal Victoria Hospital. Thankfully, I wasn't sure of the best route to the Royal. I say thankfully because it was something to discuss on the road other than a cancer diagnosis. I mean, there are lots of situations in life where you're stuck for words, but a cancer diagnosis must be in everybody's top three of 'what-the-fuck-do-I-say-here?' The consultant had given us a letter marked 'urgent' for a spine specialist at the Fracture Clinic. Why the Fracture Clinic, I don't know. But the spine specialist named by the consultant wasn't on duty. In a packed reception area devoid of chandeliers, I asked the woman behind the desk, who neither looked nor dressed nor smiled like an air hostess, what I was supposed to do. She told me and my father to find a seat. So we did.

This was about midday. At around seven that evening, my father was seen by the doctor on duty. There seemed to be only one doctor on duty. I hadn't bothered looking for the list of consultants on the walls. At half nine – nine and a half hours after we stepped through the door – we were directed to a ward.

The next few days were a series of blood tests and further scans. My family waited on the results. Before that, though, my father was moved to a private room on another ward. Not a good sign. On this new ward, a mumbling, scary man wandered the corridors. He had a livid scar running from the bridge of his nose over the top of his skull and down to the back of his neck. In a room opposite my father's, another man lay on a bed with both his legs amputated. Further down, a notice on a door read 'Special Investigations Unit'. No, this was not a happy place.

So it proved. The doctor eventually came to see us on the Friday night. He asked my father if he wanted to be spoken to alone or with the family present. My father told this young doctor to go ahead and say what he had to say. Picking his words as carefully as if he were negotiating stepping stones across a river, the doctor said that nothing was definitive as yet, that oncology had to be properly consulted and that a biopsy still had to be done, but judging by the scans, my father had a mass on his lungs which had attached itself to his spine.

Silence. Not the kind of peaceful silence that 'comes dropping slow', not 'dropping from the veils of the morning to where the cricket sings'. No, this silence was dark. This was sinister; this was deathly.

My mother spoke first. She clung to the biopsy, the fact that it hadn't been done. She asked about it but chose the wrong word. 'Doctor,' she said. 'When *is* the autopsy?'

We all laughed.

Even my father laughed. But that was a measure of the man.

There wasn't going to be much laughter from then on.

In fact, there hasn't been much since he died, either. I miss him. I miss our arguments about politics. I miss his good humour. I miss his optimism. In all his days, I never heard him say a bad word about anyone (except politicians, of course). I miss the sound of horse racing as soon as you came into the house and him screaming at some 'bastard' jockey who'd cost him a yankee. Yeah, I forgot jockeys: politicians and jockeys.

He was an intelligent man. He was brilliant with numbers. If anybody needed a bet totted up in the bookies, they asked my father. He was a reader as well. It was very rare that he didn't have a book in his hand. Worked all his adult life in a factory, though. Left school at twelve to pick potatoes. The educational reforms after the war came too late for him. I think he'd have done very well with a proper education. I don't know what he might have become. I suppose future generations will wonder the same things about their parents when university education is made impossible for the working classes once again. That's if we have future generations; if the world isn't blown up first by some crazy, dead-eyed moron who manages to get his hands on some nuclear weapons. Talking of which, my father hated Trump. I've heard it said that terminally ill people can sometimes fixate on something. In my father's case, it was Trump. I honestly think this was some kind of attempt to come to terms with his death, that he wouldn't be sorry to say goodbye to a world so messed up that Donald Trump could be President of the United States: 'How the fuck did America, the country of John Kennedy and Franklin Roosevelt, elect that ignorant slabber, that buffoon, that... that... *bastard!*' I knew the end was nigh when he stopped taking an interest in Trump. I remember telling him that Steve Bannon had been sacked and he just turned his head and looked at me vaguely. 'Steve Bannon,' I said. 'They gave him the heave-ho.' My father barely grunted, too loaded on painkillers to know what I was saying.

I miss my da.

When I was doing sonnets with 9H, I read 'When All the Others Were Away at Mass' by Seamus Heaney. Of all Heaney's poems, it's my favourite. It's about the death of the poet's mother and how he remembers her. What he remembers is one particular Sunday morning when the rest of the family were at church and he helped his mother peel the potatoes for dinner:

> They broke the silence, let fall one by one
> Like solder weeping off the soldering iron:
> Cold comforts set between us, things to share
> Gleaming in a bucket of clean water.

I asked 9H about that soldering simile. I love that line. It's so discordant and should be so wrong, and yet that's why it's so right. For me, it grounds the poem, like the bucket of clean water. It refuses cheap sentiment, which makes it all the more heart-rending, like Heaney's other great poem about death, 'Mid-Term Break', about the death of his younger brother.

As I say, I was discussing the simile when, to my horror, I found myself tearing up. I needed a moment and stepped out to the corridor to gather myself. 9H were none the wiser when I came back in, and I got on with the job without making a fool of myself, and set them a comprehension on the poem for homework and, as the man said, broke that butterfly upon a wheel.

I broke it on a wheel. I took that beautiful collection of words and feelings and turned it into a mind-numbing exercise. Because that's what teachers do.

But more and more, with each passing day, I'm unhappy with what teachers do.

Or with what I do.

This is a constant refrain, but lying on that hospital bed today, looking at my companions on the ward, thinking of my father, of time passing, of what's important and what's not…

They finished their tests. Thankfully, they were done puncturing me with needles. Eventually, the doctor came to see me.

He smiled thinly.

I girded my loins.

He told me I had late-onset asthma.

# 14 MARCH

Back to school with my inhaler. What a trooper! There should be a brass band playing and a podium where I am presented with a medal. Instead, I lost my form-class free class. What I mean by that is I don't have a form-class, and so I'm free those first fifteen minutes of the day when most other teachers are calling rolls and giving out dinner tickets, or bollocking the arse off somebody because the dog ate their school shoes or their tie. It's a blessed fifteen minutes where you try to get your head round the day ahead. Except today, I lost those fifteen minutes.

Why didn't I get a form-class? Some kind of glitch this year. As I said, I got emotional over Heaney's 'When All the Others Were Away at Mass'. I got emotional over not having a form-class, too, but it was a different kind of emotional. For as well as that oasis of peace in the morning, it also means I don't get pupils from my form-class sent to me when they've been acting up in another class. The idea is I'm responsible for my form-class; they're my team and I must make sure they're on their game (their game being table-hoops, by the way, or bingo; nothing requiring too much exertion). So if they get sent to me because they've been acting up, I have to talk to them, discipline them, whatever. Thing is, you're usually teaching another class at the time. It's an ass-ache you could well do without.

Besides all that, though, the real benefit of not having a form-class is you don't have to go on school trips. Last year, when I did have a form-class, we went to M&D's amusement park. Now, M&D's amusement park is in Motherwell, and Motherwell is in Scotland. That's a different country to the one I live in. And to emphasise this geographical separation between my country and Scotland, just to drive the point home, there's a sea between them. Maybe it's OK to nip back and forth over the French–Spanish border or the Italian–Swiss border if there's a comely senorita or milkmaid on the other side of said border, or for business purposes. Maybe. But generally, I don't think it's ever a good idea to visit another country and come back on the same day, especially when that visit involves the use of a boat, and especially – *especially!* – when the ostensible purpose of such an excursion is not for sex, and not for making money, but for – and I use this word very advisedly – fun. And to visit that other country across the sea, and come back on the same day, with a hundred to a hundred and fifty kids in tow? I say again… *fun?* What does this word 'fun' mean? Shall I look up this word? To whom would this idea of fun appeal? To the grinning, slobbering lunatic whose idea of a good time is to pop a dog in the microwave while frenziedly whacking off to videos of autopsies? I don't recognise this word 'fun'. Personally, I think that the person who organises this kind of 'fun' trip should be strapped to a chair and have their eyes pincered open, à la *A Clockwork Orange*, and be made to watch, for instance, the DUP annual conference for the rest of their life (which might well mean for the rest of eternity, because it wouldn't surprise me if it's playing on a loop down in Satan's basement as well).

Anyway, anyway, the trip to M&D's meant we had to meet up at school at 4:30 a.m. – *4:30!* – to catch the Stena link at 6:30. We got to the 'fun' park at eleven that morning and left at 5 p.m. to catch the Stena again. We arrived back at the school at eleven that very same night. Mumbling, incoherent, shell-shocked, eyes rolling in our heads, we got off the bus like we'd just returned from 'Nam, man. And that was only the teachers. I made it home as the hour struck midnight. I'd been awake for twenty-one fucking hours so a load of kids could stuff themselves full of fucking shit then puke up on a fucking roller-coaster.

Another memorable outing was to Dundonald Ice Bowl one Christmas. We had only been there fifteen minutes when a pupil slipped and broke his ankle. I spent the rest of the day in the A&E of Ulster Hospital. Undaunted, unafraid, un-fucking-believably, the school returned to the Ice Bowl the following Christmas, where the kids spent only a marginally longer time on the ice before another pupil fell over and this time broke his leg in three places and almost severed an artery. Note: this wasn't while the boy in question was performing a triple axel somersault. Like the rest of the pupils on the trip, the boy didn't know anything about ice skating. He was just given a pair of skates and told to get on with it. On those grounds of the lack of training or preparation – though what you were supposed to train or prepare on if you didn't live beside an ice rink, I have no idea – the school was successfully sued by the boy's parents.

Did I tell you how much I hate school trips?

But, boy oh boy, I love them when I don't have a form-class.

Last Christmas, on school trip day, this time to a cinema in Belfast – thankfully, finally, someone had seen sense – I was happy as Larry while I drove to work, thinking teaching was a great job altogether as I contemplated an empty, pupil-less building and a day to be spent getting paid for reading the paper and farting like a dog. Then a question popped into my head which almost made me lose control of the wheel. I pulled over into a garage. I rang the school and told them I'd been held up, that I'd be a half-hour or so late. I then bought myself a coffee and had a smoke. See, I realised I had been guilty of some very sloppy thinking that morning. For once, optimism and high spirits had got the better of me. The dangerous question that popped into my head? What if I were to get to school and they were a teacher short? What if someone who hated school trips as much as me had pulled a sickie? I'd have to go in their place, wouldn't I? Seriously, I really wouldn't want to be put in such a position. I don't know if I could trust myself to behave with any sort of dignity or self-respect. I think my disappointment would be such that I would do something desperate, like simply shit myself on the spot and pull my trousers down and show everyone, pupils and all, the contents of my knickers, just so I wouldn't have to go on the trip. Anyhow, I waited at the garage until I was sure that the coast was clear – that is, that the buses to Belfast were on the M1, packed with moaning schoolkids who had already seen the film they were going to see because they'd downloaded it illegally – then I drove into work.

If I haven't said it before, I'll say it now: you need your head on in this game.

So, as I say, I lost my form-class free class. Never mind. I logged on to my computer and found that I'd only lost one of my other frees, instead of the usual two – things were looking up! – and put to the back of my mind the important question I would have to answer during that free: whether to have a suck on my inhaler or have a smoke, or both? Then I pulled up my emails. There was one from the Principal. She wanted to see me to discuss the lesson she had observed.

This, of course, during my free.

Between the inhaler and a smoke, it was now a no-brainer. I had two cigarettes before I went in to see the Principal. She was all bonhomie. 'Hi,' she says.

'Hi,' I says.

She then apologised for not getting back to me sooner about the lesson. I demurred. She told me to take a seat. I took it while she opened her file. I noticed there was a lot of writing there. 'So,' she says, 'how do you think the lesson went?'

I had a flashback to years before. This must be their standard opening question. I answered as I had done back then. 'Yeah,' I said, 'I thought it went well.'

She nodded sagely. 'How do you mean?' she said.

I shifted in my seat. 'Well, the main aim of the lesson was for the students to put themselves in the mind of a character, to remember that a character has to somehow come alive on the page. So they have to think through the emotions of the character and imagine themselves in a similar circumstance.'

'Yes, they were supposed to be scared in the story. You told them to draw on a situation where they had been scared. You asked them what fear felt like and you asked if anyone had been in a car crash or had an accident. Some of them talked about their stomach feeling funny and their skin being cold.'

This Principal was really on the ball. It wouldn't be wise to underestimate her.

'Yeah, Fiona talked about a taste in her mouth,' I said.

'Yes, that it was like an iron taste.'

'That's right.' I shrugged. 'I thought they were very responsive.'

She didn't comment on this but wrote something in her file. 'When they re-wrote the pieces of work – because these were first drafts you were commenting on – did they improve?'

Fuck it. I gave the honest answer. 'Some did.'

'And some didn't?'

'No, some didn't.' I thought of Haley and Cathal. 'Some are not improving, no matter what I do.' There it was. I had said it. She could make what she liked of it.

She looked up from her file. 'What are we going to do about that?'

I looked at her. I liked that 'we'. Despite myself, I was beginning to warm to this woman. There was no rubbish. She was straight to the point and I felt like getting to it as well. 'I don't know what we're going to do about it. It's the teacher's curse, isn't it? You try this, that and the other and you still seem to end up at back at square one with some kids. Have you got any ideas?'

'I have actually,' she said. 'I'm going to advertise for the services of ex-teachers in the area. We have no money – they'd be doing it gratis – but I'd like to see if I could get a few of them to come in for maybe an hour or so a week and do some one-on-one reading with pupils who are really struggling. What do you think of that?'

I told her I thought it was a very good idea. There were a lot of ex-teachers out there sitting on their hands, many of them bored stupid. 'You can only play so much golf,' I said.

'Exactly,' she said. 'And it's a stupid game anyway.'

'Yes, it is,' I agreed. I hate golf; golf and tennis: knocking a wee ball about for four fucking hours.

The Principal closed her file. 'I thought it was an excellent lesson, D_____,' she said. 'I enjoyed it. The pupils did too. That was obvious. They were engaged, and your whole emphasis throughout was on praise for what they had done but also where they could improve. I also liked that there were no bells and whistles. It just felt like a normal lesson.'

'It was.'

'I know that. You also focused on vocabulary in particular. I think that must be a whole-school focus. These children don't read. We need to draw up strategies to improve vocabulary, don't you think?'

I nodded.

'Any ideas on that?'

I told her I'd think about it. And I will. She had thrown me a curveball. Not because she had praised the lesson – although a little ego massage is never a bad thing – but because she struck me as a serious, thoughtful woman, not a time-server or a bullshitter. She had disarmed me. So much so that I forgot to mention the blinds, or the curtains, or, yes, the glory hole.

With her in charge, maybe there is hope for this place.

She's not perfect, though. Not once had she asked me how I was.

She wasn't *that* thoughtful, said wounded, bleating little me, as I wondered if there was just time for another smoke before next period started. And fuck my asthma.

# 20 MARCH

The International Day of Happiness!

You wouldn't think it to look at 9C first two periods. Then again, maybe they were thinking the same, looking at me.

In a way, my day was the story of two pupils I pulled out of class to have a wee word with, as they say. The first was Vinny. Vinny's a thirteen-year-old male. When I write that, it makes him sound like an ape. I didn't write that by accident. He spends most of his time in class either grunting or scratching himself. When he looks at you it's with a wary alertness, his head slightly tilted forward, his gaze scraping the line of his brow. Listening to him, as well, when he thinks you can't hear him, there seem to be only two things on his mind – food and fucking. I don't think he's doing any of the latter at the minute, but when it happens, my money's on very little pillow talk or foreplay, the action being short and snappy, and the lucky lady in question being taken none too gently from behind.

Anyway, there he was today, ten minutes into class, sitting

in all his simian glory with neither a book nor a pen in front of him despite being told twice to get a shift on.

I pulled him out.

I gave him the spiel: that I was sick of this, tired of his attitude, blah blah blah… blah blah… blah. I finally asked him what the problem was. He scratched his balls. He actually did. He gave his balls a good meaty scratch as he looked left and right, as if to see if there was anything more entertaining than me on the corridor, like ropes he could swing on.

'Well?'

'I don't care,' he grunted.

'Don't care about what?'

'English.'

'So learning how to communicate properly doesn't matter to you?' I could well believe this was true of Vinny; a vocabulary of a hundred words or fewer would probably suffice for all his creature comforts.

'Nope,' he says. 'I only care about Art.' He didn't say this in any Wildean, declamatory way, while imagining himself grandly tossing the end of a long flowing scarf over his shoulder. Instead, it was said in an I-hate-everything-and-I-only-hate-Art-marginally-less kind of way.

'Are you any good at Art?'

He shrugged. 'I'm all right.'

'But you enjoy it?

'Yeah.'

'Why?'

Another shrug. 'Just do.'

'And what do you hope to do with Art?' Needless to say, there was another shrug. 'I mean, do you hope to be a designer, or work in animation, for instance?'

'Don't know.'

'And you don't care?'

The fourth shrug and counting. 'No.'

This was the part where I was supposed to give that other spiel about how, no matter what Vinny hoped to do, he would need an English qualification; that it was the minimum necessary for almost any kind of a decent job; that Shakespeare and Emily Brontë and auxiliary verbs might bore the tits off him, but they were only a means to an end, and that end was securing some kind of a future for himself instead of rutting about in the undergrowth and eating bananas with their skins on.

But I didn't give that spiel because, in that moment, I didn't care either. It was a waste of breath. He wasn't listening and I was only going to bore myself as well as him. Instead I told him that whether he liked it or not, he wasn't going to sit in my class and do nothing. Either he went back in, got his books out and got on with what he was supposed to be doing, or I was sending him to his form-teacher.

His choice.

So he went back in and got his books out. For the remainder of the class, he didn't do much. Then again, neither did I.

Jordan was the other pupil I pulled out. This was in the

afternoon. It was a cover class, and they'd been set work, which they were doing quietly enough, except for Jordan. Jordan was making this buzzing noise as he drew on his arm. The buzzing noise was supposed to be the sound of a tattooist's needle. Twice I asked him to desist. Twice he ignored me.

In the corridor, I asked him what he was up to.

'I'm doing a tattoo,' he said, and he held up his wrist, upon which he had drawn a watch. If a five-year-old with Parkinson's had drawn it, I wouldn't have known the difference.

'It's not a tattoo,' I said. 'You're just drawing on your hand with a blue pen and, what's more, you're disturbing my class.'

'It's a tattoo,' he persisted.

'Jordan, I want you to tell me that you're going to go back into class and get on with the work you've been set.'

'I'll do it after I've finished my tattoo.'

I could live with this on one condition. 'Does finishing your tattoo involve making that irritating noise?'

'This noise?' he says while he made the noise.

'That's the one,' I said. 'If you can finish your tattoo without making that noise and then get on with your work after, that's OK by me. How's about that?' The International Day of Happiness had been a long day. But it was about to get longer.

'But that's the sound of a tattoo,' says Jordan.

'Does that mean you're going to make that noise?'

'It's the sound of a tattoo. When you get a tattoo.'

I looked hard at this boy. He was starting to get a bit of a reputation. I'd seen his name on staff emails lately where he'd been sent to Room 5. Room 5 was for pupils who had been completely out of order. It was manned by the Principal or another member of the senior management team.

I changed tack. 'What's the fascination with tattoos?' I knew the fascination: every dickhead had one.

'They're cool.'

'Supposed to be painful, getting one.'

'Ah,' he laughed. 'It'd be funny.' That's the word he used: 'funny'.

'Yeah,' I said, 'about as funny as cancer.'

He was puzzled by this. 'Cancer's not funny,' he said.

'I know cancer's not funny,' I said. 'Neither is somebody scraping away at your skin with a needle. That's not funny either.'

Yet he was genuinely perplexed by the phrase I'd used. 'But why would you say cancer is funny?'

I sighed. 'I was being sarcastic, Jordan.'

'That's not sarcastic,' he says. 'Sarcastic is...' He tried to think of an example of sarcasm. I could see his hair wilting as his brain sucked in extra protein. He looked down at his feet and then gestured to them. 'Sarcastic is: "Look at my beautiful white shoes!"'

Jordan's shoes were black and I could see what he meant. At the same time, I'd come this far.

'That's not sarcasm,' I told him.

'Yes, it is,' he said, and he gestured to his feet again. 'Look at my beautiful white shoes!' He repeated it, this time wondrously, as if he were Dorothy in raptures about her ruby slippers: 'Look at my beautiful white shoes!'

'No, Jordan, if you were to say, "look at my shiny *black* shoes", I said, 'that would be sarcastic. Why would it be sarcastic? Because your shoes are not shiny. Your shoes are splattered with mud. Isn't that right?'

'And my shoes aren't white, they're black,' he responded.

I held up a hand. 'No, no, listen, will ya?' I took a breath. 'Y'see, sarcasm usually points out the difference between how something should be and how it actually is. It's like...' I searched for a good example. I could imagine my own hair wilting. I know my soul was. 'Like if I go to a restaurant, and I get a really terrible meal, and somebody asks me about it and I say, "Oh, it was lovely." That's sarcasm: the difference between how something should be and how it actually is. You've got muddy black shoes and so you say, "Look at my shiny black shoes!" Better still, you say, "Look at my shiny shoes!" Saying your shoes are white only confuses the sarcasm and makes it just...' The word was 'stupid' but I never use that word. 'Sarcasm has to be quick and direct. It has to hit the mark. It shouldn't make you think twice. That's why it's called the lowest form of wit. You can't complicate it. White shoes complicate it. Do you understand?'

I had to check myself. This was actually a conversation I was having in the middle of the corridor, with the noise building in the class I had left unattended. How had I got from tattoos, and this boy acting the bollix, to here? Where was I going with it? Did I even know what the fuck I was talking about? Yet, to give him his due, Jordan seem to be considering all this. He opened his mouth to respond, then closed it, then opened it again. His hair had been sucked dry. It was going to catch fire. Finally, he says: 'But cancer's not funny.'

Oh, for fuck's sake!

He had won.

'I know cancer's not funny, Jordan.' I hung my head and died just a little more inside. 'I know it's not funny. I shouldn't have said that.'

'Cancer killed my uncle.'

The way he said this. Not 'My uncle died of cancer'. He had made cancer active rather than passive in the sentence. He had used that lethal verb. I could have done a class on the difference between those two sentences. Once a teacher, always a teacher. It also suggested this was still very raw. 'I'm sorry to hear that,' I said. 'You were close to him?'

'Aye, he was round our house all the time.'

'He must have been young?'

'Thirty-six.'

'Jesus!' I said.

'He didn't smoke or anything.'

'A death like that can be difficult to understand.'

'Wreck your head, sir!'

Sir. The first time he had used the word since we'd started talking. I had singularly failed with Vinny earlier in the morning and by this circuitous route, more by luck than anything, I had made some connection with Jordan. The kind that's like gold dust for a teacher. The kind that makes the job feel worthwhile. It also means I might have easier dealings with him in future if I play my cards right. That might sound a little mean; it is a little mean. But the job being worthwhile and self-preservation go hand in hand.

'Y'know, if you're ever feeling a bit … y'know, a bit down about your uncle, you can come and talk about him. About how you're feeling.'

He nodded. 'That's all right,' he says.

I waited a few seconds. The noise from beyond my door was reaching boiling point, like there was a bunch of DUP in there who had found in their midst a gay Muslim environmentalist who was in a civil partnership with a Catholic.

'So, how about this tattoo business?'

Jordan went back in and got on with his work.

And that was my International Day of Happiness.

# 25 MARCH

Patricia is new.

She moved to our school two weeks ago. For the first week she kept her head down, never uttered a peep, sat alone. Second week, I saw her starting to talk to a few of those around her. Now, in her third week, she's loving it, a permanent smile fixed to her chops. She seems a different girl, now so confident that today she told me she didn't like using 'sir', that she'd rather call me 'dude'.

I kept my face straight. 'Don't call me dude, sister,' I says.

'Sister?' she says.

'Call me *The* Dude.'

'*The* Dude?'

'*The* Dude,' I told her. 'I want the prefix.'

It was lost on her.

Anyhow, since she's only just arrived, I couldn't set her the class assessment. Instead, I had to come up with something else. I gave her an abridged copy of 'The Monkey's Paw', that ancient horror yarn about the old man and woman who are given three wishes. She read it, but didn't agree with the ending, where the old man revokes his second wish that his dead son be brought back to life. 'I'd have wanted to see him even if he was a zombie – even if he'd been caught up in all that machinery and was torn to pieces – I'd have wanted to see him, if he was a relative of mine. So would anyone, wouldn't they?' Patricia had just articulated the dark heart of much of the horror genre. I told her to go read Stephen King's re-write of 'The Monkey's Paw', 'Pet Sematary', or she could watch the remake in cinemas at the minute. I told her I thought she'd find it more satisfying than W. W. Jacobs's hoary old tale.

But she wasn't finished. She expressed similar dissatisfaction with the premise of the story. 'Why would you wish on a monkey's paw when you've just been told the wishes all turn out bad?' That's human nature, I told her. We take risks, make mistakes, and always think that because it's us, it'll somehow turn out different even though we know, deep in our hearts, it won't. I asked her to put herself in a similar situation. 'You'd make a wish, wouldn't you?' I said. 'Imagine the monkey's paw was just sitting here on this desk in front of you and, at any moment, you could pick it up and make a wish on it.'

She shook her head. 'Nope, I wouldn't pick it up.'

'C'mon, Patricia,' I says. 'You wouldn't wish for the most beautiful, richest, most intelligent, most interesting person in the world to fall in love with you and pledge their undying devotion?'

She shook her head again. 'Nope,' she says. 'He'd probably have gonorrhoea.'

I blinked a few times. 'What do you know about gonorrhoea?'

'Miss W_____ was telling us about it in Biology, and if I made a wish on the monkey's paw, that's what Mr Wonderful would have, I'm telling you.' Patricia was starting to sound like someone from *Mrs Brown's Boys*.

'OK,' I continued, undeterred. 'What if you could have enough money to fly off to your penthouse suite in New York one day, your condominium in Los Angeles the next day, your tropical island the next day, your…?'

'Sure, I'd be knackered!' This was definitely a *Mrs Brown's Boys* sketch and, contrary to how I feel about that sitcom, I was really beginning to enjoy Patricia.

I threw up my hands. 'So there's nothing?' I said. 'Nothing in this whole wide world that would tempt you—'

She held up a finger. 'There's one thing,' she said. 'And I wouldn't care what happened after.'

She had me hooked. 'Go on,' I says.

'I'd wish there was two kinds of schools, dude,' says Patricia.

'*The* Dude.'

'OK, *the* dude – two types of schools, right?' Her teeth were gritted, her eyes were blazing, her smile was suddenly gone; no one could doubt her conviction. 'One kind of school where you put all the bullies and leave them there to bully each other … and another kind of school for the nice people!'

There wasn't much reading between the lines needed.

Presumably, Patricia had arrived late in the year because she had had enough, or whoever was at home had had enough, of whatever was going on in her old school. It explained her first week: the little mouse sitting quiet and alone with her head down, waiting, just waiting, to become the butt of some joke.

And it also explained the change in her.

I don't think this school will ever get a greater recommendation!

Though it might well get a greater recommendation than Geraldine's work. While Patricia was to do her assessment on 'The Monkey's Paw', the rest of 10P were still working on a first draft of their assessment on *Stone Cold*. To remind you, the title is: 'What makes the opening of *Stone Cold* interesting and engaging?' We've been at this three bloody weeks and this is what Geraldine has come up with:

The person who wrote Stone Cold was Robert Swindells. The story is about a teen-age Boy who became homeless and went to London to find a job and a Home but became Homeless in London as well and there's a crazy killer on the lose. The Book introduce us to a teen boy called link and a killer Shelter, yes this dose wanna make me read on because the book is really good and its just not like other books. The first thing links says is you can call me link. Yes the novel is like someone talking to you. Yes Because He lives outside in the cold and We live inside with heatin and all. He means people when people walk past me they don't see me its like im invisibe to people. Because they don't want to give money to Him. Sad Because ther still people after all Nothig diffret They just Have no Home a should just stop and Hand them some change it would Help them out. Sometimes if I only Have notes but if I Have change I would stop and give them it yes the author is trying to tell us we should treat Homeless the same as Non Homeless people Because it is still Happen There is still Homeless people getting treated like that. No it sounds like he is being sarcastic abut it. Yes it makes me want to read on.

There lifes sound the same because They both Havent got much Mates and they both as Trying to Who He is and Shelter is using a differ Name Because He doesn't want to get reconised. Yes it is short. No because He doesn't want to get caught it tell us He has got them were he wants them yes I want to read on to see what Happens.

Defolity Not link is nice and Shitler is Not. We learnt that we Need to treat others the way we want treated I would like to read on to see what Happens after these two chapter.

Shitler?

*Shitler!?*

A couple of questions. Whose fault is this? Is it mine? Has Geraldine lost so much respect for me as a teacher that she thinks she can hand in any old shitler? Or has she become so disaffected that she's handing in the same to every teacher?

Should I come down on her like a ton of bricks, eat the face off her, for such a lazy effort? I mean, the essay was supposed to be constructed to follow a series of questions. I went through these questions and the answers to them extensively, repeatedly; ad nauseam. 10P were then told that if they answered these questions with some thought and in full sentences, and ran these sentences together, they would have the basis of a decent essay. However, Geraldine hasn't even bothered to hide the fact that she's answering questions, and has written 'yes' and 'no' throughout her response. For that alone, never mind the fact that she clearly hasn't re-read a word she's written, she deserves a right bollocking.

Yeah, I should go down her throat. I should get her to re-read it and re-write it, and tell her for a start that if I see so much as one capital letter where it shouldn't be, I'm going to photocopy her response and send it home and see what they make of it there.

And will any of that frothing at the mouth do any good?

In Geraldine's case, it probably will do some good. She's better than this. How the hell could she be any worse? Yet her piece suggests a seriously worrying lack of focus and concentration. In the year before she begins GCSEs, her attitude isn't close to what it needs to be. But she will improve with even a modicum more application. Please, God!

Then I turn to Cathal. Remember Cathal? I told you, no matter how many times I go through this rigmarole, I keep getting nowhere with him. I told the Principal the same. What's that Einstein said? 'Insanity is doing the same thing

166

over and over again and expecting different results'? But what if there seems no alternative but to do the same thing over and over again? What if you are locked in that insanity with all your wits about you? A Catch-22 is defined in the dictionary as a situation in which a desired outcome or solution is impossible to attain because of a set of inherently contradictory rules or conditions. Is Cathal himself the inherently contradictory condition against which my desired outcome or solution is impossible?

The succeeding paragraphs of his essay continued just as with his introduction, with an absolute disconnect between what he was thinking and what he was writing. To top that, the writing itself was practically illegible. Once again, I'm lost for what to do. For instance, to bring this back to basics, do I spend as long as it takes on handwriting and build from there to try to make some – *any!* – kind of progress? Next year, Cathal will begin his GCSEs, studying Shakespeare, Steinbeck (if he can stay awake), Heaney and so on. How does this child regard that prospect? Schools witter on about pastoral care, but what will constant correction, constant failure, do for Cathal's mental health? If you were him, wouldn't you kick off? Is there no better way? Education is failing Cathal as it is failing so many. In his case, alarm bells should have been ringing a long time ago, long before he reached secondary school, and resources poured in to help him. This is not to dump on primary schools; they're teaching thirty to thirty-five pupils in a class. No, it's years of underfunding in education, the same as in health and welfare. The consequence? Switch on the news.

By way of Haley, the other pupil I lumped in with Cathal in a previous entry, whose work is equally troubling: I haven't seen her in the last few weeks. She hasn't been in. Perhaps non-attendance explains some of her issues. Or, conversely, maybe her attendance is so bad because she no longer sees the point.

Regarding Cathal, though, he never misses a day.

If I were to use the monkey's paw and make a wish for Cathal and his education, how could this possibly turn out any more fucked up than it already is?

# 28 MARCH

Today granny took me to the zoo
There were lots of animals like
6 marvellous monkeys
7 scary spiders
3 grizzly gorillas
1 lazy lion
2 terrible tigers
10 beautiful birds
4 cute camels
8 cuddly koala bears
9 sleeping snakes
5 giant giraffes
Then the zoo gates shut
And we went home to bed.

Terry wrote this in response to an exercise where I had asked 9C to write a poem for children. There were two specifications to the exercise:

1. The rhyme should teach a small child something
2. It should have a simple rhythmic quality

I suppose this does have a simple rhythmic quality. The first specification, though, is more problematic. I asked Terry what it was supposed to teach a small child.

'About animals,' he says.

'What – that they exist?' I swear, I'm getting more sarcastic the older I get. Jordan should be here so I could hit him with this zinger. By the way, I'm not only sarcastic with pupils. A colleague put up an email yesterday. She had arrived back in her classroom after the weekend to find a brand-spanking-new whiteboard had been installed. As she put it, though: 'I haven't the baldiest notion how to work the thing.' I emailed her back: 'I've got one too. You just write on it with a felt tip. Ohhh... you mean an INTERACTIVE whiteboard? Haven't got one of those... or blinds, or curtains, or...' (I know, I must be a dream to work with.)

Anyhow, back to Terry, who was looking at me even more blankly than usual.

'What does it teach them about animals, Terry?'

'The kind there is in the zoo.'

'Right,' I says, with a funereal sigh. 'What about counting? You do realise that if you repeated this to a child, then the child would think the first number was six rather than one, the second number seven rather than two? They'd be counting to five, rather than ten, with ten coming after two. Did you write this to confuse a child?'

Terry himself looked confused.

'Why did you begin with six rather than one?' I pressed.

'It was the first number came into my head,' he says.

I swear to God!

I had set this exercise completely on the hoof. I had a double with 9C. We were supposed to be discussing 'persuasive language' and I had photocopied an advertisement for a child's car seat. I was all ready to go, and I looked at them... and couldn't face it. I simply couldn't face another hour of mumbled replies, of silence, of their general couldn't-give-a-fuckery.

It's almost April and I have made very little connection with this class. I've said before, I don't like them. I don't mean individually; I mean as a collective. There have been classes that I've hated. Most of those, though, were head-bangers, and everybody else hated them, and they probably even hated themselves. 9C aren't head-bangers, though, they're just... depressing. Their form-teacher has gone on 'stress-related' sick leave. I wouldn't be surprised if they're a lot of the reason, rather than those other classes he might teach where discipline is an issue.

9C are the top class in their year. In any top class there'll be three or four pupils who are extremely able and they usually set the tone for the class. Often, more than the teacher, they create the work environment. That may seem contrary. Surely the teacher sets the tone and creates the energy in a lesson? To an extent, yes. But put it like this: if those top pupils in that top class are doing all their homework, responding in class, are very eager and very willing to learn, then the teacher always has a go-to and that creates a transferable energy. If, on the other hand, these top pupils are not doing homework, not responding – if their general attitude is 'What are you looking at me for?' – the teacher, no matter how well prepared or how stimulating the lesson, is often left high and dry. There is no energy, and the bar slowly gets lower and lower because it's getting heavier and heavier. Teachers are human: as with anyone, they like to get out what they put in, or at least 50 per cent of what they put in. If they're not even getting that, especially with pupils who have a lot of ability, it can be extremely dispiriting.

On my student practice, many aeons ago, I spent two weeks in a primary school. I loved it. Why? I would argue that in a primary school you absolutely get out what you put in, nine times out of ten. There's no self-consciousness on the part of the pupils; there's no 'too cool for school'. Every day, those kids are waiting for the teacher to put on a show. It can be exhausting, but it can be exhilarating too. If the teacher's up for it, there is lift-off. Not so at secondary level, especially when those kids you are banking on react like you're waving a picture of Boris Johnson under their noses. Take Cassie (please do!). Today she has no books with her. She tells me she forgot them. I make the obligatory noises; she does the obligatory shrug. Maybe Cassie will grow to be a wonderful young woman and a credit to her family, but at the minute, she is a charmless and irksome teenager who also finished top in the last assessment. When it comes to tests, she will perform; when it comes to class, she won't. And if *she* won't...

Take Terry (again, please do!), the child-confuser. Terry finished close to bottom in the last assessment. I say again: the energy levels in a class act by osmosis, and if those at the top aren't exactly killing themselves, then not many others are going to be busting their balls either. Is Terry going to write anything other than the first thing that farts in his head when he clocks the enchanting Cassie and her sloth-like exertions? It's the question of mixed ability I considered in a previous entry: success rests on the assumption that the 'stronger' pupils will pull the 'weaker' ones along. It's the trickle-down theory of education. But what if – as with the trickle-down theory of economics – those at the top are pushing rather than pulling?

To return to the exercise, I've done this before with other classes, mostly first-year, often toward the start of the year to put them at their ease, for a bit of craic. I was looking for the same with 9C: trying to find something with which we could have some fun, maybe have a laugh or two, see each other in a different light. But as with all lessons involving 9C this year, the class settled to a soporific nullity.

Eventually a hand went up. It was Tom at the back.

'Yes, Tom?'

'What's the WALT and WILF for this, sir?'

WALT means We Are Learning Today and WILF means What I'm Looking For. I'm meant to put WALT and WILF at the corner of the board at the beginning of the lesson to illustrate what the lesson will be about and what the pupils should understand by the end of it. (I'm always tempted to write MILF rather than WILF just to see how long it will take anyone to notice. Then again, there's a teacher down the corridor who has written 'We are Learning Today' and 'What I'm Looking For' on his whiteboard, rather than their abbreviations. He called me in to show me. 'Why didn't you just write WALT and WILF?' I asked. Giggling, he pointed to the bottom of the board, where he had written 'We All Now Know' – i.e. 'WANK'. He then spent periods explaining soberly to his classes how he was taking WALT and WILF one step further. So far, after a full six months, no one has rumbled him.)

'The WALT is … um…' There was no real WALT. As I said, this was just supposed to be a bit of craic. 'Children's rhymes,' I blagged.

'And the WILF, sir?'

The WILF was 'Finding a spark of life in 9C' but I could hardly say that. Now I was past caring. 'Fun,' I said.

Tom looked round at all those happy, smiling faces, his own coupon similarly euphoric. 'Fun?' he said.

'What, Tom?' I said, brandishing a dictionary, my voice rising. *'You need to look it up?'*

# 29 MARCH

A day to forget.

There I am, standing outside my room, saying hello to 10P as they troop in. All as it's supposed to be. Then Joseph in the room opposite comes out and we exchange some back and forth about the football. He's a big Spurs fan and thinks they stand a chance in the Champions League. I'm partway through bursting his bubble when suddenly there's a scream from my classroom like somebody's been knifed. I rush inside. Debbie is in floods of tears and holding her hand. It seems she and May had been tussling over a seat. Why? I have no idea. All my seats are the same. There are things in life to disagree over – the kind of beer that goes best with a curry; if those are Jürgen Klopp's real teeth; the method by which Bono should be executed – but what you set your ass down on in my class is not one of them. Anyhow, the upshot is that Debbie's hurt her thumb. She goes off to the nurse. I've pretty much forgotten the whole thing – a little TLC, a hug from the nurse and Debbie'll be right as rain – when the head of third year comes in to tell me Debbie has gone home. 'Where were you when it happened?' says the HoY.

I look at him. When it happened? When *what* happened? What are we talking about here – 9/11? I'm getting a sinking feeling. 'I was at the door, where I should have been,' I told him. 'They'd just come in.'

'D_____,' says yer man in a whisper. 'I had a look. I think her thumb's broke.'

'You're fuckin' kiddin' me!' My exact words.

The HoY makes a face. 'I don't know for sure,' he says. 'She's in a lot of pain, and when I told her to try and move it, she couldn't.'

'What'd the nurse say?'

'She's recommending the parents take her to Casualty.'

The HoY left. I sized this up. If Debbie had a broken thumb, I was in shit. Even if it was only some kind of sprain, I was in shit. I could only hope that it was neither, or that Debbie's parents were the kind of people who understood that shit happens, because if they decided to sue the school... It looks bad. Pupil has her thumb broken in a classroom. First question: what was the teacher doing? Oh, he was in the corridor talking about the footie.

I mean, I've come across worse situations to try to explain. I remember a colleague wandering round his classroom with a staple gun in his hand while he corrected a comprehension. Some boy got an answer wrong, and my colleague puts the staple gun to the back of his head mock-execution style and pulls the trigger... *and puts a staple in the lad's head!* He thought the stapler was empty. Next thing, white as a sheet, he rushes into my room to see if I have one of those little staple-removing tools and tells me what happened. So there we are in his room while he tries to extract the staple from the boy like the back of the boy's skull is a bulletin board, all the while telling me and the class, 'Sure, it could happen to anyone, couldn't it?' He was trying to make a joke of the whole thing – at one point, he even said, 'Nurse, could I have a little more light, please?' – but he was absolutely bricking it, a look on his face like he'd been asked to smile for the camera but had been hit by lightning instead. As I say, imagine trying to explain it. 'Well, you see, your honour, it was like this: I had this staple gun in my hand and I thought it was empty...' And the upshot? He got away with it. He could easily have lost his job but his luck was in. It transpired that he had put the staple in the right boy's head, because any other boy might have run home crying to Mommy, but for whatever reason, this boy didn't. That was the end of the matter. It was never spoken of again, except on those occasions when my colleague and I had a few drinks and nearly bust a gut laughing about it. It was one of the funniest things I've ever witnessed. Not at the time, though.

But in all my years of teaching, I've never been accosted by an irate parent. I've never been hauled into a Principal's office to explain myself. So far as I know, I've never had any kind of complaint made against me.

'There's been a complaint against you.'

This is break-time. This from the SENCO (Special Educational Needs coordinator). I sigh and curse Joseph across the corridor, who really shouldn't have distracted me when he did. It's all his fault, the bastard.

'It's broke, then?' I says.

'What is?' says she.

'Debbie's thumb.'

'What about Debbie's thumb?'

'This isn't about Debbie's thumb?'

'Who's Debbie? What about her thumb?'

'Forget it,' I says. 'What are you talking about?'

'Jason in 8D,' says the SENCO. 'His mom was in. She says he doesn't get enough English homework.'

This is 8D of the interminable, soul-crushing twenty-five minutes to see if everyone had their homework done. 'Did she come in to specifically complain about me?'

'No, it was a general meeting. She said the same about Maths as well.'

As I've said before, homework is a parent's first line of defence; it's not their fault young Billy is a bollix, it's the school's. Yet, I will admit, I have been lax with 8D and homework of late. In a court of law she would win. But, today of all days, I don't want to be thinking about courts of law.

'Right,' I tell the SENCO, 'I'm on it.'

'And what's this about Debbie's thumb?'

'Forget it,' I tell her.

I wish I could.

By the afternoon, I haven't heard anything. At least the

Principal hasn't come to see me after a phone call from Debbie's parents. No news is good news. Or is it? I stop 10P in the corridor. 'Anybody hear anything about Debbie?' I ask lightly, jovially. None of them have. There's nothing by the end of the day, either.

Except word that the Principal wants us in the staffroom for five minutes.

Fucking hell, what next?

What's next is that the bastards are back! The bastards being the Education and Training Inspectorate. They're coming in for a four-day visit the week after next. I love that word 'visit', don't you? That's the word they always use, like they're just dropping in or stopping by. Like an old aunt who smells.

Staff are all taking this in when the HoY from this morning taps me on the shoulder. 'I rang Debbie's house,' he says. 'She's fine. They didn't even go to Casualty.' He shrugs. 'Just a sore thumb. Bit of an over-reaction.'

I want to tell him that he was the one who fucking over-reacted.

But I don't. I've had enough unpleasantness for one day.

I just go home.

# 4 APRIL

Strange one today. A colleague of mine in the English department gives me a pro forma about standardised marking schemes but accidentally also passes me a story she had been marking. Here it is:

Finz-Lolapalooza was eating power sorses like a boss in the too-warm sea where polars bears starved and zeezaks swim and extractid joy out of killing rocks in the cracks of the tumbling glaciers. That was until Cuddles showed and covered them all in ash that covered the sky and the yellow ball of nightime and daytime so that all that was left was slime green. 'Oh Barnsley!' Cuddles cried, 'a feest of plump energy fit for a hungry god like me who's eyes are too big for my belly'. But Finz-Lollapaooza changed into a froot-pop in an electric re-boot, lightning and ice in it branches, glowing on the bed of the far-too-warm brown sea now like radation, comunicating by telekinetic until even the nme Zeezaks joined him in a revolution when they all saw that all of the polars bears were dead and the sea-lions were next. So they all proseeded to exist eternally in the emptiness of the universe that Cuddles had created and was sick of now until Cuddles sneezd and an egg pooped out from between her big ears. 'Oh Barnsley' she whooped, 'looks like I created another universe! Maybe I can do lots better this time.'

And so it ends.

I don't know about you, but I think this is kind of wonderful. I can imagine a very young Anthony Burgess writing something like this. 'Eating power sorses like a boss' – what a simile! '[E]xtractid joy out of killing rocks in the cracks of the tumbling glaciers' and 'too-warm sea where polars bears starved': how's that for an environmental statement? And the God in this dystopia, in 'the emptiness of the universe', who has blotted out the sun is called Cuddles. If that isn't irony, I don't know what is.

Oh Barnsley!

There's talent here. There is. This is someone who sees the world differently, who is looking for a new angle. Isn't that what an artist does? In my book, whoever wrote this is more of an artist than somebody who calls themselves one after holding a tune for two minutes on *The X Factor*.

Yet if I had to strictly mark this according the 'Communication Levels' by which we standardise our grades, I would struggle. Strictly concentrating on spelling and grammar, it wouldn't get any higher than a Level 3, which is mid-stream Primary 7, i.e. a half-decent ten-year-old. Maybe that was why my colleague accidentally passed it to me, because she'd been puzzling over the marking scheme while she tried to assess this piece of work against it. I'll have to ask her when I next see her but, yet again, it's one of those anomalies which can make a mockery of the system.

And talking of mockeries of the system, it's Thursday, and the inspectors 'visit' on Monday. I'm humming The Smiths' 'Panic'. Yet why all this panic? The staff have declared themselves 'non-compliant' – that is, the inspectors can go fuck themselves. If they enter the classroom, they are to be handed a directive from the union that reads: 'Following a ballot for legitimate industrial action, I have been instructed by my Union that I am not to co-operate with ETI at present. I have been directed to cease teaching in your presence; however, I will continue to supervise the children as normal.'

So, again, what's the panic?

It's just the fact that they are coming. They make everyone uneasy even if they aren't watching our lessons. If they were watching our lessons, it would be proper panic. Why? What's to fear? Are we all shit-bad teachers just waiting to be found out? No, we're not, but the fact is that even the best teachers can teach a bad lesson. Maradona wasn't always shit-hot, with defenders tumbling in front of him like skittles. I saw him shank a few volleys into Row Z; Messi and Ronaldo the same. Anybody can have a bad day – a bad couple of days, even.

The best teacher I ever had – and by best, I mean most effective – was a Maths teacher. She taught me from first year through to third. The reason she was so good was because you knew exactly what you were getting every lesson. First thing, she corrected our homework. Next, she explained a maths problem on the board, with her doing all the talking and us doing all the listening. To conclude, she set us an exercise on the problem for homework. Next day, same again: we corrected the homework, she did a problem on the board… That was it, every lesson. It was like a metronome. You could have set your watch by where she would be in any lesson: fifteen minutes in and she would have corrected the previous night's homework, twenty-five minutes gone and she'd be setting the next night's homework. She put our class through what were called RSA exams. By the end of third year we had all passed RSA Stage 3, the equivalent of an O Level, two years ahead of time. I thought this teacher was brilliant and so did everyone else. However, if today's ETI had sat in on those lessons, she'd have been torn to pieces; they'd have been picking over her bones before five minutes were up. They'd have wanted to know why she hadn't divided us into groups, or why she hadn't set us the maths problem to solve ourselves, or why we weren't correcting each other's homework, or why we were all sitting singly and in rows, or why she did all the talking, or why she didn't teach the lesson while hopping on one leg with a calculator balanced on her head so all the visual learners in the class could have something to look at (I'm joking about this last directive, of course, but I'll get back to the general principle).

I had an A Level teacher whose classes I loved. If my old

school had a Hector, the good guy from *The History Boys*, this man was him. We were meant to be studying the English Revolution but often the class would consist of a discussion of the newspaper front pages and editorials. He wanted our opinions and our ideas. He would ask us what books we were reading. That was his big thing. If he didn't consider our reading matter stimulating enough, he would provide an alternative from the stacked shelves behind his desk and tell us to write a precis of it for class discussion. He would call any book he particularly recommended 'a feed of a book': 'Here's a feed of a book, young D____,' he would say to me and the rest of the class as he flung *Troubles* by J. G. Farrell across the room, or R. H. Tawney's *Religion and the Rise of Capitalism*, or Robert Tressell's *The Ragged-Trousered Philanthropists*, or *Strumpet City* by James Plunkett. 'We don't need any more accountants and solicitors; we need writers and we need thinkers – people who are going to lead this country out of slaughter.' I distinctly remember reading those books and this is over thirty years ago. That was the kind of impression this very clever man made on me. I remember another recommendation: Frantz Fanon's *The Wretched of the Earth*. Reading it was like light pouring into a dungeon room. This was a brilliant but unorthodox teacher, and one with a missionary zeal, who encouraged me to explore the world of ideas, and to believe that I had ideas myself and what I had to say might be worth listening to. I was just starting out as a teacher, just out of college, when I heard he'd been shunted off into early retirement after an inspection. I smiled when I heard that. He would have alto-gether rejected the premise of someone judging his lessons and probably told whoever turned up at his door what he thought of them and their methods. I could imagine him reaching for a book from his groaning shelves, some philo-sophical work on the base folly of subjectivism maybe, and telling the inspector that if they really wanted to learn some-thing, they should read that book or, if they preferred, they could stick it up their jacksie. No, I don't think he'd have played ball. I like to think that he quite simply told them to fuck off and that's why he was given the push. But that's the romantic in me.

He died recently, my History teacher; him and another teacher in my old school who he was best mates with. They died within weeks of one another. They were an unlikely pair, absolute chalk and cheese: one a thin, ascetic intellec-tual with a vague resemblance to John Lennon, the other a huge bear of a man who everybody called Uncle, even us lot, the kids (even the Headmaster, I think). He taught wood-work, except it had just been renamed CDT (Craft, Design and Technology) when I started the school. I remember him giving off about this – the change of name, not me starting the school – and I also remember a mini-speech he gave which was the exact reverse of Robin Williams's in *Dead Poets Society*: 'Aye', he says to a class of us, speaking in his thick country accent, 'all of them writers and Shakespeares and Dickenses and all are great boys, but who put a man on the moon, eh? It was the fellas who know how to do stuff;

it's the fellas who can do and not just write about doing it
– them's the boyos!' I got an A in my CDT O Level. I ran
into Uncle in the corridor the following year and he gave
me a well done and then said: 'And you haven't feckin' hands
to bless yourself!' For those unfamiliar with the idiom, this
didn't mean that I wouldn't say my prayers, it meant that
I was useless with my hands. He then told me that there
had been fifteen or twenty better joiners in the class than
me but all the examiners and inspectors were interested in
was people who could write a few decent pages on how to
construct a chair or a table, not the actual construction of
a chair or a table itself. 'It's all paperwork now and theory.'
He really was raging, and I seemed to be the focus of his ire.
'It's all changing and it's all feckin' bullshit! It's not the doing,
it's the seen to be doing!' With this, he chuntered off down
the corridor, leaving me, a gauche sixteen-year-old, slightly
shaken.

*It's not the doing, it's the seen to be doing.*

When it comes to the inspectorate, I would heartily
concur with Uncle. From the boxes that need to be ticked to
the freshly photocopied schemes of work and lesson plans
that must be neatly laid out, to the playing of 'bingo adverbs',
or the dramatisation of Alfred Noyes's poem 'The Highway-
man' as a police interrogation scene, or the splitting of the
class into 'crews' to devise raps on the characters in *Macbeth*.
This is the kind of shit that goes on when the inspectors
pitch their tents. For fuck's sake, I once had a colleague who
spent two weeks rehearsing a lesson – *rehearsing!* – where

he lined the kids up to represent forms of speech – nouns, verbs, adjectives, punctuation marks and so on – and chore-ographed this troupe of bewildered children to form simple, compound and complex sentences. He had me sit in on this as a trial run. I don't know what he expected me to say, but I was speechless for all the wrong reasons. I emphasise, this was a perfectly good teacher, very well-respected, but he was simply in a complete flap at the thought of the inspectors.

'Whom the Gods would destroy, they first make mad!'

It's a circus. The only things missing are fire-breathers and lion-tamers. I was going to say clowns, but the teachers are the clowns. The thing is, too, the inspectors know this is all a show and a sham. They know none of this – or very little of it – goes on day after day but, hey, in the words of Michael Corleone, 'We're all part of the same hypocrisy.'

It's not the doing, it's the seen to be doing.

Wise words from old Uncle, God rest him.

# 8 APRIL

I'm in the computer room. My class are leaving, another class lined up to come in. I say a hello to Turlough as he leads his class in. 'How'd you get on at the weekend?' he says. I'm taken aback. I don't know Turlough well enough that he could presume to ask me questions about my sex life, or lack of it. I play a straight bat. 'How do you mean, Turlough?' I say.

Now *he's* looking at *me* funny. 'The Grand National – did you get the winner?' he says.

'Oh!' I smile. I can be quite the dickhead at times. 'Nah, Turlough,' I tell him. 'Horses are not my thing.' And they aren't. In fact, I'd go so far as to say that if the world's most famous steeplechase was being run past my window, I would probably close the blinds. (That's if I had any blinds. I'd pull the curtains, too, if I had any of them.) My father was fanatical about horse racing and placed a bet every day. Just a few quid, mind. We never went without shoes or food because of his gambling. But his love of the gee-gees was all-consuming. That's OK these days with laptops, phones and half a dozen TVs in most households. Not so fine, though, when there was only one TV in a house, and you were a kid, and you wanted to watch a film or a cartoon or basically any-fucking-thing other than horse racing. Even on FA Cup Final day, that blessed day of the year which was the only chance we got to watch a live club match, the match would have only just started and my da would be telling us to knock it over for two minutes for the 3:15 at Kempton, or whatever. Year after year, in a match that could never live up to the billing, and which was invariably settled by one goal, my brother and I would miss that one goal and instead find ourselves watching ridiculously named equine beasts being flogged to death by half-grown men to the sound of my father turning the air blue and telling us how he could have bet the winner, except some bastard so-and-so at the bookies had put him off it.

So, no, horse racing's not my thing. I was sickened of it a long time ago.

This doesn't put Turlough off, though, as he proceeds to tell me how he did each-way bets on the runner-up and the fourth-place horse, and how he also won the school sweep (of which I was not a part).

I congratulate him on his superior mental acuity.

'Did you make any money at the weekend?' he says to a passing pupil. This girl looks even less interested than me and walks on.

I escape Turlough and memories of FA Cup Final days of yore. Besides, I shouldn't have been hanging about. The inspectors weren't visiting classrooms, but they were on the corridors, and all staff had been advised – ordered – to meet and greet their classes on time to minimise disruption or any kind of altercation between lessons.

The day passes smoothly enough, though 8D are extra hyper for some reason. They're going to be mustard come second year. By third year, they'll be off the Richter. Jason, he of the parent who put in a complaint about lack of homework, is in 8D. I set the whole class a nice, juicy long homework, on account of their general bolshiness (which is only storing up future trouble for myself given the class's abysmal track record but, hey, 'Tomorrow is another day', as another malcontent once observed), and then give Jason an extra exercise. Jason rears back like I've waved a shitty finger under his nose. 'Ask and ye shall receive,' I say to him, before telling him that he'll maybe think twice the next time he wants to make excuses as to why he's not being fast-tracked to an Oxbridge placement. I don't think he quite understands the reference but it gives me great pleasure saying it.

As I say, the day is passing smoothly enough – except for when it comes to my insides. All morning, I've been hobbled by a series of gastric explosions. At first I thought it was diarrhoea and practically sprinted for the bathrooms in between first and second classes while leaving the classroom assistant in charge. This would normally be a strict no-no with the inspectors lurking, and the CA wasn't happy about it, but it was an emergency. I made it to the bathroom and yanked down my trousers just in time for a genuinely unearthly noise to escape my extremities. Anyone passing on the corridor might have heard it and gone to a window to see if the sky had suddenly darkened. Sweat broke on me. And tears. I mean, this actually hurt, hurt like hell, like someone had just ripped off one of those hair-removal strips from the tender hairless meat of my bum-hole. Within seconds, the smell was unearthly. On occasion, I've gagged and retched at someone else's flatulence, but never at my own. I do so now, while feeling for my buttocks just to make sure I haven't lost sections of them in the blast. Looking between my legs, I see the water in the toilet bowl is still rippling from the disturbance in the air, but there is no deposit. It was merely trapped wind. I say 'merely', but there is nothing merely about this. A half-hour later, I'm aware of trouble building again, like someone has a tight hot fist around my colon, and this time disappear into the store and proceed to rattle stuff about to cover the noise of the Krakatoa-like detonations in the South Java regions below my belt. I pray no one follows me into the storeroom, which now has a whiff of the charnel house about it. Of course, this is all extra embarrassing for a teacher. Like the Queen of England, we don't do these things. I presume the corgis have taken no end of abuse over the years regarding their gaseous proclivities while Elizabeth Windsor looks on as if butter wouldn't melt. If we teachers have to drop one, we will wander around a room, stealthily discharge well away from our desks and then move on, leaving those at the back of the class to blame one another while we open windows, wave at the air and generally fulminate about today's youngsters and their fast-food diet which is doing nothing but damage to their intestinal tracts. If I'm feeling particularly bold, I'll even pick out some boy – never a girl; that would be too cruel – who has fecked me off recently and point the finger of blame. However, such Machiavellian mischief is impossible in this case; these farts are just too incendiary. At home, I'd be recording them; in school, I'm terrified I'll follow through. Any other day, I might cry off sick, but I can't do that with the inspectors in. Still, what if I do follow through? What then? Let them write that in their report. 'In the view of the ETI, wholesale evacuation policies must be re-examined, and we don't just mean with regard to the fire-safety policy...'

By midday, however, the emergency is almost over. I no longer feel like I've just had a gastric band fitted and decide against driving home for a new pair of pants. Then, first after lunch, there's a polite tap on my door. I think it's the inspectors when the door opens and the Principal pops her head in. 'Can I see you for a second, Mr K_____?' she says.

I follow her into the corridor. Her face is like stone. She looks under pressure. No doubt the inspectors aren't helping. Then again, she was one in a past life. I don't feel any sympathy, even though she has shown flashes of humanity in my previous dealings with her. 'Something wrong?' I say, while simultaneously reassuring myself that it surely couldn't be anybody complaining about the smell.

'Did you have a conversation with Mr M_____ about the Grand National this morning?'

This was an odd question and my expression must have registered such. 'It wasn't a conversation,' I tell her.

'No?'

'It was a monologue. Turlough did all the talking. I hate horse racing.'

'Horse racing and golf. You said you hated golf in our meeting, remember?' she says, off my puzzled look. 'I take it you're not a sporty person?'

'I like football,' I said. Had she really pulled me out of class to discuss my sporting preferences?

'Anyway,' she continues, and sighs. 'Look, there's been an allegation made against Mr M_____ by a pupil who claims that he insinuated that she was a prostitute.'

'*What?*'

'Yes. But Turlough claims that the girl has taken this completely wrong, and that he was talking about the Grand National with you at the time, that he was referring to the horse race and the remark was entirely innocent.'

'What remark?'

'The girl says that he asked her if she had made any money at the weekend.'

I copped on right away and started to laugh. 'Yeah,' I said. 'He was talking about the race. And she thought…?' I laughed again.

Finally, the Principal had to allow a smile. 'Thank God for that,' she said. 'As if I don't have enough on my plate today. Thank you.' She walked off and I waited until she had turned the corner before I let loose with another horse-and-cart, though this was merely an after-shock; a slight tremor compared to the tectonic plates that had shifted earlier in the day. Nevertheless, I gave my leg a good shake and took the requisite thirty seconds for the smell to disentangle those invisible threads that cling to the offender, and returned to my room.

I got the whole story from Turlough later. Like much else in teaching, it was both funny and it wasn't, because this wasn't simply a case of the girl in question going to the Principal and telling her what Turlough had said. Rather, the girl had run home and told her mother. Why the girl leapt upon such a remark and acted in such a way, I don't know. Then again, I had taken him up wrong myself when he first addressed me that morning. Anyhow, when Turlough went to the office, he was confronted by the irate mother who threatened him with the police and promised she would have his job for this. Not surprisingly, he was stunned, and according to him the worst thing about it all was that he hadn't the first fecking clue what she was talking about, even when he was told what he had said. His brain frozen with shock, he had completely forgotten about his conversation with me and he sat there in front of the Principal and absolutely, resolutely, denied everything. Meanwhile, the mother was practically foaming at the mouth and asking why her daughter would make up such a thing. This seemed like a pretty fair point and there were four or five heart-stopping minutes of this potentially career-defining confusion before Turlough's brain clicked back into gear and finally, at last, he remembered talking to me.

Case closed. Apologies all round.

Being a teacher: it may make you question your sanity at times – it will certainly make you question your life choices – but it's never dull.

And sometimes it smells.

# 11 APRIL

Yesterday, astronomers captured the first image of a black hole. The picture shows a halo of dust and gas, tracing the outline of a colossal black hole at the heart of the Messier 87 galaxy, 55 million light years from Earth. The very thought of it, both the engineering that went into the photograph and the object of the photograph, is truly stupendous and breathtaking.

An unimaginable distance away, this black hole sits like God's eye, as if watching us, waiting for us.

I discussed it with 9C: its demonstration of the way in which Einstein's general theory of relativity leads to surprising and counter-intuitive conclusions in extreme situations. How when an object comes into contact with such phenomena, all hope is lost, and that object is dragged inexorably towards destruction; how that object becomes trapped in a spherical ellipse, going round and round in ever-decreasing circles, causing a shattering instability and deformation from which there is no path of escape. As such, these ever-growing, ominous masses are terrifying beyond reason: no living features appear to be observable, and all is darkness within them, just as everything becomes very dense when they are approached. The first thing that happens within proximity to them is that bodies and minds are pulled asunder and time seems to slow, perhaps appearing to stop altogether. They are warped and warp everyone around them. They distort reality beyond recognition. They manifest their energy in very conspicuous ways but shed no light. They have no role or function other than negativity. They have mass, but no charge or momentum. Some of them, particularly noisy ones, are called dumb holes. Because they have only a few internal parameters, most of the information about the matter that went into forming them is lost. In fact, no one really knows how they were formed, due to insufficient data. This information can be thought of as existing inside them, inaccessible from the outside as information that enters them is gone for ever. Consequently, much about them is puzzling. They are considered a curiosity and an enigma. Although we understand enough to interpret some observations of them, there are still many mysteries about the details. Deep inside them, in the regions that cannot be directly observed, there lurks a basic mystery. Hence, what can we know of their true nature? The only thing we can really say for sure is that there is some kind of collapse and depletion in their central core.

But enough of 9C.

# 12 APRIL

Geraldine has completed her third draft of her *Stone Cold* essay. I'll remind you of her first draft:

The person who wrote Stone Cold was Robert Swindells. The story is about a teen-age Boy who became homeless and went to London to find a job and a Home but became Homeless in London as well and there's a crazy killer on the lose. The Book introduce us to a teen boy called link and a killer Shelter, yes this dose wanna make me read on because the book is really good and its just not like other books. The first thing links says is you can call me link. Yes the novel is like someone talking to you. Yes Because He lives outside in the cold and We live inside with heatin and all. He means people when people walk past me they don't see me its like im invisibe to people. Because they don't want to give money to Him. Sad Because ther still people after all Nothig diffret They just Have no Home a should just stop and Hand them some change it would Help them out. Sometimes if I only Have notes but if I Have change I would stop and give them it yes the author is trying to tell us we should treat Homeless the same as Non Homeless people Because it is still Happen There is still Homeless people getting treated like that. No it sounds like he is being sarcastic abut it. Yes it makes me want to read on.

There lifes sound the same because They both Havent got much Mates and they both as Trying to Who He is and Shelter is using a differ Name Because He doesn't want to get reconised. Yes it is short. No because He doesn't want to get caught it tell us He has got them were he wants them yes I want to read on to see what Happens.

Defolity Not link is nice and Shitler is Not. We learnt that we Need to treat others the way we want treated I would like to read on to see what Happens after these two chapter.

Here's her third draft:

The author of Stone Cold is Robert Swindells. The narrative is about a teenage boy who becomes homeless and travels to London to track down a job and get a house but he ends up being homeless in London too and there's also a demented killer on the loose called Shelter. I want to read on to see if Link dies or he survives.

The first thing Link says is, 'You can call me Link'. The novel is conversational, like someone talking to you. I feel bad for Link because he's only a teenage boy who lives on the street and most teenage boys and girls have a warm house to come back home to and he has a doorway. When Link says, 'They don't see me, it's like I'm invisible' he means no one gives him anything they walk right past him with their head down. It's distressing because he's still a human being after all. I think Link is being ironic saying, 'Hang about and I'll tell you about my fascinating life'. His life is far from fascinating, he has nothing and I don't think he is overjoyed with it. It makes me want to read on to hear about his life. Shelter's life is different to Link's because he has a home and food and money but Link has none of it. Shelter is trying to keep out of sight and disguise his identity so he changes his name. Shelter used to work in the military. We know this because he says, 'Get fell in my lucky lads'. This is what they say in the army to get people to line up. I want to read on and find out more about Shelter and about what is going to happen to both of them.

Link is definitely nicer than Shelter. We learn from this book to treat people the way they want to be treated. I want to read on to see what happens after these two chapters because Link is a really civil and affable person and I want to determine if he dies or if he's going to be unharmed. The chapters are so short and leave the story on a cliff-hanger so the reader can't wait to find out more.

It's far from perfect but Shitler's gone, at least. That's one positive. Then again, there are many positives. While unsophisticated, the grammar now does what it's supposed to do and helps rather than hinders the piece and, for the most part, it no longer reads like the answer to a series of questions. Yet what I'm really pleased with is the vocabulary. Or some of it, anyhow.

A few weeks back, the Principal spoke to me about vocabulary, and she brought it up again at a staff meeting recently. She wants vocabulary strategies in place across all subjects and argued this was vital if results are to improve. There's no such thing as an inaudible groan but that best sums up the reaction at the meeting.

My reaction? Whisper it, but I think she's right.

Armed with a thesaurus, vocabulary was the main thrust of Geraldine's third draft. That's my strategy, to take a final concentrated pass on any extended piece of work with word choice exclusively in mind. Note the changes: 'story' to 'narrative'; 'find' to 'track down'; 'crazy' to 'demented'; 'talking' to 'conversational'; 'sad' to 'distressing'; 'happy' to 'overjoyed'; 'army' to 'military'; 'nice' to 'civil and affable'; 'see' to 'determine'. 'Sarcastic' also became 'ironic', sarcastic having been introduced in her second draft.

I particularly like 'determine', though. If Geraldine can get it into her head to use 'determine' instead of 'see', that alone makes the exercise worthwhile. Yet how much smoother the piece reads with just this light sprinkling of better words and phrases.

Of course, this can backfire. Children can often easily misunderstand a word form when using a thesaurus. A girl in 8D, instead of 'starting to eat her breakfast', is 'commencement to eat her breakfast'. But hey, you can't make an omelette without making a total shit of the kitchen, and for children who do not read, something has to be done. And that's the problem – they simply do not read; it's as alien to them as truth and selflessness are to Boris Johnson (and the Tories in general). If you do not read and the vast majority of your communications are with people who do not read, then how can your vocabulary improve? I would estimate that the vocabulary levels of most children I teach has not advanced since Primary 5 or 6. At age nine or so, they are familiar with a bank of words which serves their day-to-day experience. By then, external stimuli, i.e. books, become surplus to basic language needs, and vocabulary ossifies and takes on an *otherness*; it becomes elusive, a series of 'big words'.

For how this plays out as an adult, think of Donald Trump, a man who famously doesn't read, and who rambles from one half-finished brain-fart of a sentence to another simply because he runs out of words to finish the sentences. Qualifying and explanatory clauses tumble into one another for the same reason. Why? Because he has no vocabulary. Take 'stupid' out of his lexicon and he would struggle; remove 'bad' and he would be tongue-tied; add 'moron', 'loser' and 'cheeseburger' to the banned list and he would be speechless. OK, OK, I'm taking the piss, but let's listen to a man who obviously thinks a thesaurus is a breed of dinosaur. Here he is, the 45th President of the United States, telling an interviewer that he doesn't watch the news channel MSNBC:

I never thought I had the ability to not watch. Like people think I watch 'Morning Joe'. I don't watch 'Morning Joe'. I never thought I had the ability to, and who used to treat me great by the way, when I played the game. I never thought I had the ability to not watch what is unpleasant, if it's about me. Or pleasant. But when I see, it's such false reporting and such bad reporting and false reporting that I've developed an ability that I never thought I had. I don't watch things that are unpleasant. I just don't watch them.

Seriously, what is this man trying to say here? That he doesn't watch a certain TV programme? And he doesn't watch it because it is unfairly critical of his presidency? And he has developed an 'ability' not to listen to people who are critical of him, an 'ability' – he makes it sound like a superhuman power when all he's doing is switching a channel – which he thinks does him an enormous amount of credit? Is that what he is saying? Answers on a postcard.

'I never thought I had the ability to not watch.'

What the fuck kind of a sentence is that?

Here is a transcript of an interview with Trump in the *New York Times* where he describes a dinner for heads of state:

So, it was tremendous media. And we took a picture of everybody, the wives and the leaders, and then the leaders, and, you know, numerous pictures outside on the river. Then everybody walked in to see the opera. Then the opera ended. Then we walked into a big room where they had dinner for not only the leaders – Lagarde [Christine Lagarde, managing director of the International Monetary Fund] was there, who I think is terrific, and various others. You had the E.U. people there, people other than just the leaders, but quite a few people. I would say you have 20 times two, so you had 40, and then you probably had another 10 or 15 people, you had Christine Lagarde, you had some others also.

This is truly shocking in its banality, in its base-level, monosyllabic, rambling sterility. 'Then everybody walked in to see the opera. Then the opera ended ... Then we walked into a big room...' This is *Dick and Dora Go to the Opera*, right? All that's missing is Nip the dog. Christ Almighty, this guy said this out loud. He said it to reporters from the *New York Times*. I'm tempted to put [*sic*] after every one of the sentences – or what passes for sentences – and I'm sure they were too. He must have been drunk, right? Surely to God, he'd had a few (a few JDs laced with ketamine and formaldehyde)? Except Trump doesn't drink. Alcohol has never touched his lips. Can you imagine what he'd be like hanging off the end of a bar? Can you imagine sitting beside him on a long-haul flight where he was talking to you in between knocking back double vodkas and trying to 'grab the pussy' of the stewardess?

We are used to obfuscation from politicians. We've become almost immune to it. They are skilful manipulators of language; it's part of their stock in trade, and they've been hiding behind words from the year dot. What we're not so used to is a politician who gropes for meaning and clarity like someone in a basement fumbling for the light switch while his trousers are round his ankles and shit is hanging out of his ass. Can anyone doubt that he stopped learning words at about age nine and hasn't read a book since he graduated from short trousers (probably the only thing he's legitimately graduated from)?

All in all, considering Trump, I would even go further than the Principal and argue that reading and attention to vocabulary is not only about words; it is about extending and stretching the functioning of the brain, i.e. if you don't use it, you lose it, baby. Trump himself would use that phrase. Those are all words he would know. But would he know how they apply to him when he is looking in the mirror and doing his comb-over? The answer is… y'know… let me see… these guys, they come to me and they say things to me like… like they come to me… all these people… these beautiful people… these great, beautiful people who I think are really great and terrific… like, they talk to me when they come to me like you wouldn't believe… and y'know what I say to them… I say… I say, guys… did I tell you… let me tell you… did I tell you this? It's like this, you see… it's like… it's like you wouldn't believe… then they say to me… because they come to me, these really great, terrific people… they come to me because I know things… and they know I know things… they know I know lots of things… big things… you wouldn't believe these big things I know…

*Oh, shut the fuck up, Donald!*

So, yes, vocabulary – it needs urgent, systematic, corrective action.

Again, funny enough, just like a certain person.

# 15 APRIL

I was a little late this morning because my car needed servicing for its MOT, and the garage didn't open until nine, so I rang the Principal and told her I needed to see the emergency dentist and I'd be in around ten. At five past I was passing her office and Sammy was sat there. Sammy's been in a spot of bother lately because of his less than wholesome attitude to race relations. I don't know the details, and I don't want to know, but rumour has it that he has a swastika tattooed on his back. But seeing him there this morning, waiting outside the office, brought me right back to Tristan.

I encountered Tristan eight years ago in a previous school. A girl I taught, Jennifer, was sitting on one of the chairs outside the office that morning. Tristan, on the other hand, was too agitated to sit down. I'd never come across him before, but suddenly he was right in my face. 'I'm going to be expelled!' he practically howled. This while clutching the collar of his shirt as if he wanted to wring his own neck. His eyes were like cue balls. He might have been on something. If he wasn't on something, then maybe he should have been.

I didn't want to stop and ask, but 'duty of care' and all that shit. 'Why are you going to be expelled?' I says to him.

He didn't answer, but groaned and pulled at his collar some more and went and leaned his forehead against a window. He reminded me of Cheswick in *One Flew Over the Cuckoo's Nest*, that unhinged little child-man forever on the verge of a violent meltdown.

Jennifer piped up. 'He was looking at funny pictures.'

'Funny pictures?' I asked her.

'Y'know,' she says.

I didn't know. Why had she said 'funny' rather than 'dirty'? Was 'funny' worse than 'dirty'? As in, stuff involving animals or children? And how was that funny? Tristan was now walking in dazed circles and moaning softly to himself. I decided I didn't really want to know. I'd leave this up to the Principal, good man that he was. Trying to talk to this fella would be like trying to talk a jumper down off a roof. I walked on but a classroom assistant was coming the other way. I stopped her, nodded to Tristan and asked if she knew who he was, adding that he seemed very agitated.

'Fuck 'im!' she says.

'Fuck 'im?' I repeated. I concluded from this that 'funny' did indeed mean 'children' and he'd been caught with child pornography on his phone.

Not for the first time, I was wrong.

'That's Tristan,' she says. 'He's a neo-Nazi.'

'Excuse me?'

It seems that earlier in the week, Tristan had been

extolling the virtues of Anders Breivik, the headcase responsible for the mass shooting in Norway. According to Tristan, this guy was a hero and a prophet.

'Fuck 'im!' the CA repeated as she walked on.

As the day wore on, I found out a little more about Tristan. I looked him up to see if he was on a statement. He was indeed. He had Asperger's syndrome. I've taught a few Asperger's kids. One of the classic symptoms is fixation on a certain topic. I used to teach a child who became fixated on Stephen King. And this fixation was my fault. He saw me reading *The Dead Zone* outside a café in town one summer's day. When the new school year started, I got bombarded with 'Did you know...' questions about Stephen King. Did I know Stephen King's wife was called Tabitha? Did I know Stephen King used to be a teacher? (In turn, did this little guy know that King got out as soon as he fucking could?) Did I know Stephen King's mother died of cancer? Did I know Stephen King used to be a drug addict and an alcoholic? This just went on and on until I had to take this boy out of class and talk to him, and limit him to two Stephen King questions every class. This fixation also illustrated the second classic symptom of Asperger's, which is that people with this condition are frequently unable to read social signals. Often, they have little to no empathy. This child couldn't spot that I was ready to grab him by the neck and toss him through the window. All in all, though, it was pretty harmless; a minor irritation.

Then again, there are those famous high-functioning,

ferociously intelligent Aspergians like Greta Thunberg and, supposedly, Alan Turing. The condition can give, just as it takes away. But what if someone with Asperger's didn't become fixated on Stephen King, or the survival of the planet, or algorithms, and instead took an obsessive interest in the likes of Anders Breivik, or his most recent incarnation, Brenton Tarrant, who committed the New Zealand atrocities? What if the Third Reich was their thing?

I don't know. Just saying.

Tristan wasn't expelled, though, or even suspended. I saw him in the playground later in the day. He was walking on his own, his head nudging and bobbing way out in front of him, walking really quickly like the rest of his body was trying to catch up. He looked both pitiful and unnerving. I thought briefly about trying to have a word with him but then I spotted Jennifer. As I should have done earlier, I asked her what she meant by 'funny pictures'. A few of her friends were with her and they butted in. Clare told me Tristan was a racist. Emily said that he didn't say hello, he said 'sig hail'. 'Sieg heil,' I corrected her. 'That's the one, aye,' she said. Finally, Jennifer got a word in edgeways and said the funny pictures were concentration camp scenes with 'jokey' captions. The world's changing, eh?

What was that about the arc of the moral universe, Dr King?

So why wasn't he suspended, at least? Most likely his Asperger's was taken into account. Most likely some expert on the condition came in to have a chat with him about acceptable and unacceptable behaviour. I presume that's what happened. Whether it was or not, though, at least it's good to know I don't live in a country where the likes of Tristan – or Sammy – could wake up one morning on the wrong side of the bed and simply take a bazooka, a few grenades or a semi-automatic rifle out of his father's gun-cabinet and decide to do his bit for the white race.

By the way, regarding that little white lie this morning: I got the idea for the emergency dentist because my front tooth was sore. By teatime, it was aching. Yes, that's right, I did go to the emergency dentist. Not my own dentist, the one in the hospital. Stuff it up you, says you. Anyway, I had an abscess. I thought the dentist would just send me home with some antibiotics. Instead, she snapped on some shiny blue rubber gloves and told me she had to reduce the inflammation. (Why the hell would anybody with brains want to become a dentist? One of those unanswerable questions, like: How can anyone find Jeremy Clarkson even the least bit entertaining?)

But as this dentist stood over me and drained my abscess – as the stinking, vile, malodorous pus poured from my gums – I thought of all those with deep holes inside themselves that they choose to fill with the most poisonous shit.

# 17 APRIL

Last day before the Easter break.

Video day!

And when I say video day, I *mean* video day. I mean good old-fashioned VHS. I wheel out the trusty Dansette combination TV and video player from the mausoleum that is my storeroom. First years' faces when they see it are a picture. They couldn't look any more gobsmacked if I was trailing a dinosaur on a lead. Ignoring the red sticker on the side of the Dansette that tells me I'm taking my life in my hands, I plug in Old Reliable and stick on… *Jaws*.

That's right, *Jaws*.

The boys and girls stretch out their hands towards me in base supplication; they rend their garments and pull at their hair; the wailing and gnashing of teeth can be heard down the corridor. '*Jaws*! But…' 'Wha? *Jaws*!' 'No way!' '*Jaws*? I mean… *Jaws*!'

Ignoring these piteous cries, I press play on my video copy of the movie, which I have had in my possession for, oh, maybe thirty years, and for the first two or three minutes or so there's still much grumping and groaning until, as if by magic – and I suppose it is magic – you could hear a pin drop. For the next two hours, the children are totally immersed in the story.

Works every time.

It is amazing. Anybody who wants to know how to make a brilliant movie, watch *Jaws* over and over and study every beat. I love the story about a test screening in a packed cinema. Spielberg was standing at the back of the auditorium, watching the audience rather than the movie. By the end of the screening it was obvious to everyone that this film was going to be huge. Studio executives were clapping Spielberg on the back, hardly able to contain their excitement, dollar signs in their eyes. But Spielberg had spotted something: a lull. A five-minute section of the film where the audience just didn't seem as engaged as they could be, where maybe a few nipped out to the toilet, or popcorn boxes were being rattled. Refusing to accept the smoke being blown up his arse, Spielberg went home and in a swimming pool filmed that unforgettable moment where Ben Gardner's severed head pops out of the hole in the bottom of the boat.

Now, that's fecking genius for you!

Of course, I don't always play *Jaws*. I've been showing videos in the run-up to Christmas, Easter and summer breaks for twenty years now. That adds up to a hundred or more films I've screen-tested in front of a very tough audience. Any slackening in the pace, any sags in the middle of the second act, and my little darlings will begin a shuffling and a farting. Plot holes, poor characterisation: my lot will sniff them out like ferrets down a hole and there'll be a scraping of chairs, much nose-picking, requests to use the toilet and a general restlessness.

Not while they're watching the good folks of Amity Island being eaten, though.

So *Jaws*, yeah, it's the daddy. But what's number two on my list of best popular entertainment movies made over the past couple of decades judging by my screen tests?

One of the *Star Wars* movies, surely? That *The Force Awakens* one made over $2 billion at the box office.

What about the *Lord of the Rings* or *Pirates of the Caribbean* franchises?

*Avatar*, right? Or *Titanic*? Two of the highest-grossing movies of all time, both by James Cameron. Shit, he must be good for a tenner.

'No,' you're screaming. '*Harry-fucking-Potter!*' Has to be one of those Hogwarts horror shows, surely to God?

The *Batman* movies?

The *Twilight* movies?

*Frozen*?

*E.T.*?

*Indiana Jones*?

Drum roll, please… 'and the Second-Best Picture…' – judging by the quiescence and general engagement of many very hard-to-please children whose attention spans have gradually attenuated over the years until goldfish are more focused; children who are sitting on hard chairs, watching an old video, in an old classroom with a glory hole punched in the wall and no blinds or curtains on the windows (did I mention any of that before?) – 'Second Best Picture goes to… *Dumb and Dumber!*'

By a country mile. The shitting scene. The karate in the restaurant. The cop drinking the bottle of piss… the kids just lap it up (the movie, not the piss).

All of the above list were major disappointments. Sure, some kids watched some of them the whole way through, but most didn't. The original *Star Wars* was probably the biggest eye-opener. After ten minutes, nobody – and I mean nobody, not even the geeks or the nerds – was the slightest bit interested; same with *The Empire Strikes Back* and *Return of the Jedi*. I myself find them and their modern incarnations, well, total shite: overheated, reheated nonsense. So how come they make so much money? Probably because there's fuck all else on at Christmas while the latest George Lucas bore-fest is taking up four screens, that's how come.

Third best picture?

A pound to a penny says you won't get it. This didn't even make it on to the top 100 comedy movies of all time on Rotten Tomatoes, the main internet film review site.

I'll give you another few seconds.

*Mean Girls*, Tina Fey's seminal 'bitch-flick'. All teenagers respond to it and can see themselves or their friends somewhere amongst its cast of misfits.

Number four you've probably guessed somewhere already – *Jurassic Park*, which, of course, is just *Jaws* in the jungle, without those three great characters, Brody, Quint and Hooper.

Number five pains me. It genuinely makes me despair for the next generation: *The Waterboy* with – I'm not going to use the word 'starring' – Adam Sandler, a man who is to funny what Ozzy Osbourne is to bat conservation. But, hey, what do I know?

And what do I care?

It's Easter!

# 29 APRIL

The end is in sight.

Rounding the final curve, opening our legs and showing our class, as Ron Pickering was wont to say.

First off, the Principal was able to give initial feedback on the inspection. My breath could hardly have been more baited. She described the inspectors' conclusions as 'fairly positive'. I don't know what that means. It sounds like one of those 'fairly positive' statements I might write in a pupil report, such as 'Little Johnny is *aware* of the homework policy', that is, Little Johnny couldn't give a fiddler's about homework, or 'Little Johnny is *aware* of the uniform policy', i.e. it would help if Little Johnny didn't turn up to school each day missing his tie and proper shoes and looking like he'd slept in a ditch after being chased through the night by a pack of wild dogs.

On the whole, the Principal's feedback is as clear as mud. She writes that on 'safeguarding', our 'overall effectiveness reflects broadly the guidance'. Oh, but I do love a grammatically correct sentence. But what does it mean? Again, it sounds like a Little Johnny comment. At the end of her email, the Principal thanks staff for all their 'support, kind messages, texts, late nights, last-minute information and for going the extra mile'. Reading that, I think to myself (not for the first time): did I miss something?

But there is one clear and definite upshot to the visit from the ETI: Room 5 is closed. I've mentioned it before. Manned by senior teachers, it's where unruly pupils are sent when the classroom teacher has decided enough is enough. But now Room 5 is no more; it has kicked the bucket, bitten the dust, breathed its last; bereft of life, it rests in peace. Why? I got this verbatim from a senior teacher: that the inspectorate told the Principal it should be closed immediately and that 'those children deserve an education too'.

Hooorrraaayyy!

Well-fucking-done!

I congratulate all those grand personages, who are not working in challenging classrooms day after day – and perhaps, maybe, probably, have never worked in such environments – who visited our school with the purpose of improving it, and have removed one of the main methods by which teachers can get on with their lessons in peace.

Yes, those grand personages, those mealy-mouthed fatheads; no doubt the same kind of idiots and no-nothings who sit on the Commons Select Committee for Education, which recently released a report entitled 'Forgotten Children'. This report decries the 'scandal' (scandal! 'I say, Finlay, old chap, old pip, old fruit, it's a scandal!') of permanent school exclusions, which, in England, have leapt from 0.08 per cent in 2015/16 to... wait for it... Would you Adam and Eve it? 0.1 per cent in 2016/17. That's some leap, eh? Wouldn't you agree? That's a whole 0.02 per cent. And, of course, it's the fault of teachers and schools. ('I say, Finlay, old fruit, we never had these problems at Eton. What was that – he told the teacher to fuck off? My word, if anyone had said that to dear old knobbly-cock Digby-Smythe-Cumberbatch he'd have taken them at their word, bent them over the coal scuttle, rogered them senseless and had Matron stitch them up afterwards.') Yes, it's the fault of teachers and schools, and nothing to do with rising class sizes, soaring poverty levels and reduced budgets. Cop this in Paragraph 36: 'There appears to be a lack of moral accountability on the part of many schools and no incentive to, or deterrent to not, retain pupils who could be classed as difficult or challenging.' Maybe these fools need to go back to school themselves after mangling the English language like this, but – excuse me – 'moral accountability'?

Is it any wonder I swear?

Again, only people who are totally ignorant of the practical reality of a classroom and wider school environment could come to such a crass conclusion. Exclusion itself is a last resort. If it happens – and it is extremely difficult to make it happen, such is the red tape involved – it happens for very good reason, most often because the excluded pupil has become a severe danger to themselves and others.

I came across an interesting statistic lately: that over 50 per cent of prisoners have at one time or another been excluded from school. You can look at that in two ways. Firstly, you could make the case that not enough was done for these people when they were younger, and that if schools had put the necessary time and energy into trying to help them and prevent exclusion – and been given the requisite resources to allow for this help (ah, there's the rub!) – then perhaps they wouldn't have ended up in prison. Conversely, you might ask why schools should be expected to keep these individuals in their classrooms and teach them quadratic equations and Boyle's law and conversational French when, first chance it gets to have a look at them, wider society bangs them up behind fifteen-foot walls? By the way, I'm not saying wider society is right to do that, I'm just saying that that is what it does. 'Fuck this for a game of soldiers,' it says, 'I'm not having you about the place!' Yet, if a school decides to act in such a way – if teachers, whose only knowledge of handcuffs and prison guard uniforms and restraint techniques has been gleaned from dirty magazines and websites, throw up their hands and cry foul, or if a Board of Governors, acting on a Principal's instruction, exclude someone who very shortly may be deemed so untrustworthy, recalcitrant or plain dangerous that they need to be caged like an animal and only allowed to eat with a spoon – the school is deemed 'lacking in moral accountability'?

Which brings me back to the Commons Select Committee. Note the title of their report, 'Forgotten Children'; the same forgotten children who, according to the inspectors, 'deserve an education too'.

Which brings me to my main point.

God forbid, heaven forfend, but could I just say a word or two about those other forgotten children? I believe I've mentioned them before. Y'know, the ones who aren't fucking you off to your face and whose favourite noun isn't 'cunt'; the ones who don't spend their every waking hour bullying and harassing other children and adults; the ones who don't take great exception to being told to get out their books or get on with some work; the ones who don't look like tumescent, angry cocks, with veins pulsing in their red pitted foreheads, when asked to say the simplest things like 'please' or 'thank you' or 'excuse me'? The ones who don't think it's cool to behave like total shitbags day after day and who don't create a scenario whereby young teachers feel like Nelson Mandela emerging from Robben Island when they step out through the school gates for the last time, while older teachers consider the pros and cons of a mild heart attack, which should get them six months' respite and a foot in the door of early retirement?

To repeat: What about those forgotten children?

Where's the moral accounta-fucking-bility there?

Maybe I should moderate my language somewhat, but I am tired to the back teeth of this… humbug. There, I've moderated it. And, yes, I do believe those 'difficult' children deserve an education. I do. I know that many of them have no home lives and no self-worth, that much of their aggression stems from fear and hopelessness and desperation, that many of them suffer from medical conditions over which they have little or no control… but there has to be some balance here.

A recent report from NASUWT, the teachers' union, stated that one in four teachers in the UK experience physical violence from their pupils at least once a week and nearly nine in ten said they had received some sort of verbal or physical abuse from pupils in the past year – 86 per cent said they had been sworn at and 46 per cent said they had been verbally threatened. And what is the Department for Education's response to these frightening statistics? 'We are committed to tackling bad behaviour in schools, [which] have made great strides in empowering teachers to tackle this issue and have recently announced a £10 million investment to support schools to share best practice in behaviour management.'

There you go, then – problem solved!

But let's just break that down a bit; let's just examine that £10 million. For a start, let's consider the number of schools in England, Scotland, Wales and Northern Ireland. How many schools is that, says you? According to figures from BESA's 2018 report, the British Educational Suppliers Association (and they should know), there were altogether 32,113 primary and secondary schools. Now, 10,000,000 divided by 32,113 = 311.40. That works out at £311.40 per school. What's that going to pay for, in this enlightened age when Alexander Boris de Pfeffel 'Man of the People' Johnson – son of an MEP and brother of a MP, descended from King George II on his mother's side – until very recently charged fifty grand a speech to rail against the Establishment, and once described his £250,000 earnings for writing a weekly column in the *Daily Telegraph* as 'chicken feed'?

Or how about teachers, and all those vast bowls of chicken feed from the Department for Education? How many teachers are there in England, Scotland, Wales and Northern Ireland? According to BESA there are 506,400 full-time teachers. If we divide this into 10 million, we get 19.74. That's right, that's £19.74 per teacher.

Maybe you're thinking I'm getting a little anal with all these figures. Funny, that, because £19.74 might buy a couple of tubes of lube. Unfortunately, due to the fact that I'm a teacher and not much of a catch – no catch at all, in fact, as I've been told on any number of occasions – I'm not au fait with the exact price of sex lubricants, but a round twenty sounds just about right for investing in these products so as to make the procedure a little less painful; the procedure, of course, being teachers told to bend over and spread their bum cheeks and smile and take whatever is coming to them. ('I say, Finlay, old chap, old pip, old fruit, maybe that's it! Maybe all these beastly working-class oiks and rotters need is a good rogering, like we used to get off dear old knobbly-cock Digby-Smythe-Cumberbatch. Never did us any harm. Quite the contrary, nothing like it for sorting out the officer class from the infantry. By Jove, Finlay, that's what the Empire was built on!')

Again, I'm sorry for the indelicate language, but it does seem an apt metaphor for what is happening in our schools, and the importance the Department for Education attaches to the scourge of indiscipline, its deleterious impact on the mental and physical health of teachers, and its effects on the education of those children who come to school to learn rather than create mayhem.

I'll return to the figures one more time, just to ram it home, as it were. Considering that the average annual budget of a secondary school in 2016/17 was £4,617,000 and the average budget of a primary school was £1,048,000, rounding it off to the nearest thousandth of a per cent, the Department for Education's investment in their behaviour management best practice initiative comprises 0.007 per cent of a secondary school's yearly budget and 0.03 per cent of a primary school's budget.

If these numbers could spell, they would spell the words 'Just fucking get on with it!'

As our school just has to fucking get on with it after the closure of Room 5.

The Department for Education, Commons Select Committees, the inspectorate… it's all ignorant head-in-the-sand lip service; it's what makes them look good in their latest report. Remember old Uncle: 'It's not the doing, it's the seen to be doing.' They only pretend to care about these 'forgotten children'; both kinds of forgotten children: the ones causing the problems and the ones suffering as a result.

Assholes!

Any of that lube left?

# 1 MAY

'Is Shakespeare dead, sir?'

'Yes, Nina. He's been dead about 400 years. But those are some of the things you can find out – when he was born and when he died.'

'I thought he was that black man.'

'What black man?'

'Y'know… that black man.'

This is a verbatim conversation between me and Nina. At last, finally, 10C had finished their assignments on *Stone Cold*. We hadn't looked at any Shakespeare so far this year and I felt there should be some nod towards it in preparation for GCSE. Nothing too taxing, though. I decided they would do a project; maybe concentrate on a few of the sonnets, each of them to pick a play and look at character, theme and so on. I'm not even going to get into whether kids should still be studying Shakespeare. The man is a colossus! No one comes close to his genius. I was in second year at secondary school when I first read Shakespeare and I absolutely fell in love with *Twelfth Night*. I can still quote long passages from that play by heart. I loved its playfulness, its humour, its sun-drenched setting, its beautiful, gorgeous optimism ('Many a good hanging prevents a bad marriage'). Looking back – this would have been, oh, 1980 or '81 – I realise now that the play was everything the North of Ireland was not at that time (and still isn't). Those were the years of the hunger strikes and the feeling that the place was tipping into full-scale civil war. Maybe *Macbeth* would have better suited the mood, but *Twelfth Night* was a welcome tonic. As I say, I loved it, and I think it was the first thing I ever read that demonstrated the importance of story-telling to our wellbeing, and not just as an escape but as a validation of our better nature. (In fact, I borrowed the VHS copy of the play from the teacher. It was a BBC adaptation starring Robert Lindsay, Felicity Kendal and Robert Hardy, and I bunked off school one Friday after-noon to watch it. Am I the only person ever, in the history of education, to have mitched school in order to go home and fill up on Coke and crisps and enjoy a Shakespeare play (and a BBC Shakespeare at that, with all its cardboard scenery)? It indicates one of two things: either I have an extremely cul-tured sensibility or... I'm just plain weird.)

Anyhow, I was explaining the project when Nina interjected.

'What black man?' I said. I know that was a silly question, but sometimes you just can't help yourself. For the briefest of moments, it passed through my mind that she might have been referring to Othello, but if Nina thought Shakespeare was still alive she would hardly have heard of that horny Moor.

Cathy piped up: 'Michael Jackson?'

'No,' says Nina contemptuously. 'Not Michael Jackson.'

I swear to God, this was the conversation. Shakespeare was a black man but he was certainly not Michael Jackson. Was the clue in the name? Y'know, Michael Jackson was not William Shakespeare because Michael Jackson was Michael Jackson and William Shakespeare was, you guessed it, William Shakespeare. But, gadzooks, Batman, no! No, the clue was not in the name because next Nina said, 'Michael Jackson's dead. This black man's still alive.'

'But Sir said Shakespeare was dead,' said Cathy.

'I know,' said Nina. She tutted and rolled her eyes in exasperation at herself. 'That black man, sir, y'know the one… I thought he was Shakespeare.'

'Michael Jackson?' Cathy repeated.

'Not Michael Jackson!' Nina exploded.

From across the room, Cathal shouts, 'Michael Jackson was white anyway!'

'Not when he was born, he wasn't, you!' The way she spat that 'you' suggested Cathy was a big Michael Jackson fan and took great umbrage at… Well, I'm not exactly sure what she was taking great umbrage at. Did she think somebody else had turned him white? (Or forced him to sleep with children?) I had to put a stop to this. If it had been a Monty Python sketch, I'd have laughed along, but in a classroom you can only take so much zaniness. 'A black man who's still alive?' I asked myself out loud. 'Barack Obama?' I said to Nina. I know, I know, but, as I say, I had to end this 'discussion' somehow.

'But he's the President,' Nina replied.

Silly me, eh?

Then suddenly she had it. Eyes wide, a big smile on her chops, she pointed a finger like a gun… '*Nelson Mandela!*'

There are times in life when you should just shut up. This was one of those times. So, of course, I opened my mouth. 'Nina, how could you think Nelson Mandela was William Shakespeare?'

She shrugged. 'I just thought everybody called him Shakespeare.'

'Why would you think that?'

'I don't know. I just did.'

'Right,' I said, 'Moving on swiftly. Oh, and by the way, Nina, I hate to be the one to break it to you, but Nelson Mandela's dead.'

'Is he?' she says with a gasp. 'OMG!'

'Yeah, they buried him and everything.'

'So who was Shakespeare, then?' she says without skipping a beat.

I couldn't compete with this. As Mark Twain might have opined, we were separated by a common language. I held my hands up shoulder high like she had a gun on me. 'Don't know,' I said. 'Some fella.'

Nina was agog. 'So why are we doing work on him if he's just some fella?'

Meanwhile, across the room, Cathal was on a two-minute delay. 'He was,' he says. 'He used to stick bleach in his face with needles.'

The mind boggles... or bubbles... or farts. This little ex-change is just a by-the-by. Light froth; we're all familiar with those internet pages full of silly things that children say. I've come across a few over the years, like when I was explaining some background to *The Boy in the Striped Pyjamas* and the persecution of Jewish people through the ages. Of course, I mentioned the crucifixion, even though the Romans were behind that one, egged on by a few Jewish bigwigs. The class were looking at me blankly. What didn't they understand? I didn't understand what they didn't understand. The crucifix-ion? Surely not? 'Y'know,' I said, 'where someone whose name began with a J was killed?' Even I was taken aback at this knowledge vacuum. This wasn't a top form, but still. A hand went up. 'Yes?' I said. 'John F. Kennedy?' ventured this girl. Then there was the class on Cromwell – I've taught a little His-tory in my time – and telling the class what a killjoy bastard he was; that even going for a walk on a Sunday, unless it was to church, could result in a hefty fine. I asked the class what they would have done on one of Cromwell's Sundays, to which this little fella at the back said he'd have no problem with that, sure, it was just like any other Sunday, and he'd have stayed in his bedroom and knocked on Cool FM. Yes, yes, I could go on: the first year who thought AD meant After Dinosaurs; the fifth year – *fifth year!* – who thought BC meant Back Centu-ries (seriously, I think the Religion syllabus needs looking at). Anyhow, anyway, Nina's was only the latest example of this joyful ignorance. Yet I was reminded of a more pernicious form of it a little later in the day when I went to Spectrum.

That's right, I went to one of the LGBTQ meetings in the library at lunchtime. I was curious. I asked the teacher in charge if I could pop in. The more the merrier, she told me, but also advised me to talk to the kids in general about why they were there without asking straight out how they identified; that Spectrum was about providing a supportive environment where people could talk about how they felt rather than feeling any pressure to label themselves as this, that or the other.

I counted forty-two present. I was told numbers had held very steady from the first week. A lot of those I talked to wore 'Ally' badges. I thought of my old schoolmate with the 'ABBA' badge. I was told that an ally is simply a friend of a person who is LGBTQ and not LGBTQ themselves. In fact, most of the room were allies. The rest of the room, or the ones I talked to, who wanted to talk to me, designated themselves 'non-binary'. That seemed to be the main classification: someone who identified as neither male nor female. No one described themselves as gay or lesbian. I talked to Tracy, who said she was non-binary and pansexual, which meant that she was attracted to people regardless of their sex. I asked the difference between pansexual and bisexual. She said I was confusing gender and sex. Bisexuality was about sexual attraction, pansexuality had nothing to do with sex, that it was an attraction that was gender and sex blind and that pansexual people are often attracted to other people who are non-binary.

Tracy was very articulate, and very sure of these terms and

significations, and looked me straight in the eye when she was talking to me. I was impressed by her. I was impressed by all those I talked to. Lee, an ally, said he was here to offer support because he thought it was simply the right thing to do, and quoted figures on suicide amongst transgender young people (89 per cent reported contemplating suicide with 27 per cent having attempted it). David was the same and he was helping write a script for a short play which was going to be presented at an assembly.

I take back all I said. This wasn't faddishness or coolness. These young people were sincere and there was a genuinely warm atmosphere in the room. I could see why kids wanted to come to Spectrum. There was a spirit about it, a feeling of all-in-this-together. There was a lot of laughter, a lot of conversation. It *was* cool, but in the right sort of way.

Then I asked a question. I asked it separately of Lee, Tracy and Graham (who said he was non-binary, 'though I could be gay'). The question was: what did they think about what happened to Lyra McKee?

Answer came there none.

That's right, not one of them knew what I was talking about. They all looked at me blankly. None of these thoughtful, articulate and clearly intelligent young people had heard of Lyra McKee. Now, this isn't quite on a par with Nina thinking Nelson Mandela was William Shakespeare, or that JFK was nailed to a tree 2,000 years ago... but in the context of Northern Ireland, it's up there.

Lyra McKee was the LGBTQ activist and reporter who

had been shot dead two weeks previously on Holy Thursday by the New IRA during a riot in Derry. Her death had dominated the airwaves for a week and made the front pages of the English papers. Her funeral had been attended by the Taoiseach and Prime Minister, and the officiating priest had called on local politicians to finally put aside their differences and talk to one another. He hoped and prayed that reconciliation and a new tolerance, values which Lyra McKee had championed all her short life, would be the legacy of her death.

And these kids had never heard of her.

I found that astonishing.

At the same time, I didn't find it astonishing.

Amongst this next generation, there is an ignorance and indifference about the world beyond Snapchat which is truly appalling. Frightening, even. Yes, there are exceptions, of course there are exceptions, but for the most part, they don't watch news, or read it on their phones (needless to say they don't buy or read newspapers), or talk about it. There seems a total disinterest in the world beyond their world or the world of their friends (or allies). Yes, the big stuff – climate change, gender/sexual inequality, the Third World – they know things are wrong there; but because they have no context in which to place these issues, because they don't follow news, they are and will be easily duped by the next sensationalist post on Facebook, or whatever. My friends and I grew up in a world where we knew who the Tories and Labour were and what they stood for. Whether we agreed or disagreed, we knew why the miners were on the picket line and Irish prisoners were on hunger strike. We knew about the Falkland Islands and Robben Island and Three Mile Island. We knew, and engaged with, the philosophy behind punk music and ska and reggae and weren't just singing the songs. In other words, we had context for the world in which we lived. Then again, considering what a fuck our generation has made of this world...

But I listened to a commentator on the radio after Lyra McKee's death who said the LGBTQ community was the North of Ireland's only hope. Theirs was a third way which might destroy the old tribalism of Nationalist and Unionist: they were a 'non-binary' threat to the status quo. If they could field candidates in elections on a social equality agenda, they might, just might, be able to break the log-jam which has strangled proper politics in this region (and wouldn't that be one up the arse for Save Ulster from Sodomy?).

I like to think this commentator is right, and I know there are spokespeople amongst the LGBTQ community who are an articulate, informed and forceful breath of fresh air. Lyra McKee was one of them. But the LGBTQ community needs this younger generation to breathe the same air and – for all their good intentions, for all their sincerity, for all their bravery, for all their undoubted intelligence – watch some news... read some books...

*And, from time to time, y'know, just for five minutes or so, look up from their Xboxes and PlayStations and fucking phones!*

# 2 MAY

My alarm went off at 6:30. I pushed the snooze button, and would probably have pressed it two or three more times, except my phone pinged with an email. It was a lady from a literary agency, a lady who mustn't use the snooze button on her phone. Anyhow, this was her email:

> Although I have considered this carefully, I'm afraid it just doesn't quite grab my imagination in the way that it must for me to offer to represent it. So I shall have to flow [*sic*] my gut instinct and pass on this occasion. I'm sorry to be so disappointing, but thanks for thinking of us. Of course, this is a totally subjective view, so do keep trying other agents and I sincerely wish you every success with it elsewhere.

I'd sent off the first few chapters of these entries to some agents in the hope they might then ring me up and proclaim mine 'an urgent, original new voice which must be heard'.

Most writers say they could paper their houses with rejection slips, that it goes with the job.

Still hurts, though.

I'm tempted to name and shame this lady, and therefore it would follow that if you, dear reader, have just read this correspondence, that means that this book has been published, and that eventually someone did phone me, and possibly proclaimed mine 'an urgent, original new voice which must be heard', and this lady who sends emails such as the above first thing in the morning (when they know the receiver of such a missive is just about to get up for another day's slog at the chalkface) would be justifiably pilloried in literacy circles for passing up a hot catch like myself.

Yes, I'm tempted to name this lady, except I'm not as heartless as she is. I mean, fuck's sake, tell someone they're useless at the end of the day, preferably on a Friday, when they're sitting with the consolation of a cold pint in their hand and they can put it into some kind of a perspective – not when they've just pressed the fucking snooze button!

So there I was: a literary failure, a cheap hack, a fool for thinking I could have anything interesting to say, sloping into work this morning. Then I knock on my computer to discover I've lost my frees... *again!*

This was going to be a complete bastard of a day.

Except, as it turned out, it wasn't. 10P started their Shakespeare projects and worked away dutifully, cutting and pasting from the internet, learning how to use Microsoft Publisher. By the end of the two periods my mood had lifted somewhat, even to the extent I could crack a joke with Nina about Nelson Mandela (though not the one about Winnie and his column).

Then I started a new unit of work with 8D on newspapers. I gave out old newspapers and scissors and glue and put a lot of stuff on the board – horoscope, subheading, Classifieds, byline and so on. They were to find examples of these in the newspapers and cut them out and stick them onto an A3 sheet and label them. They were happy as pigs in shite. I think they thought they were back in primary school. Would've brought a tear to your eye.

Last two was 9C. They too were starting a new unit of work: speechwriting. I debated whether to start with General Patton's to the Third Army – 'I want you to remember that no bastard ever won a war by dying for his country. He won it by making the other poor dumb bastard die for his country' – or Martin Luther King's 'I have a dream…' I love the Patton speech but King's was on YouTube and it was longer. You know my feelings about 9C. Listening to the speech in its entirety would kill twenty minutes. It was a no-brainer.

I borrowed a projector from a colleague, hooked my computer up to it and played the YouTube clip on the whiteboard, despite the glare from outside my curtainless, blindless windows. (Have I mentioned them before?) I hadn't taught the speech in years and I was struck by its power once again. The last five minutes are monumental. No one can listen to the lilting ebb and flow of King's voice, its searing passion – 'I have a dream that my four little children will one day live in a nation where they will not be judged by the colour of their skin but by the content of their character' – its glorious ascendant clauses – 'With this faith we will be able to work together, to pray together, to struggle together, to go to jail together, to stand up for freedom together, knowing that we will be free one day' – no one can listen to those words and not be stirred by them.

Not even 9C.

We were doing speechwriting as a follow-up to the advertising unit. My plan had been to give 9C a transcript of the last part of the speech and have them analyse it in much the same way they would analyse an advert. But that seemed a bit dry, a bit butterfly on a wheel, after the fervour of what we had just listened to; blasphemy, almost. Instead, I decided to talk through the transcript. It was the right decision. Suddenly, 9C were using all the key terms I'd been trying to teach them these last few months: Michael spotted the positive aspirational language, '... this nation will rise up...'; Claire spoke of the alliteration which contributes to the rhythm, '... the sons of former slaves and the sons of former slave owners...'; Stephen saw the metaphors and figurative language: 'heat of injustice ... heat of oppression' contrasted with the 'oasis of freedom and justice'. In fact, 9C got it all – the personal testimony, the emotional language, repetition, the rule of three, buzzwords, rhetorical language.

And I was as fired up as them. I told them about my visit to the Lincoln Memorial and of the museum dedicated to King's speech which is in a room under the memorial. I told them I was with a group of other people and a tour guide, a white man in his fifties. He was bursting with pride, waxing lyrical about King and his speech and freedom and justice and how that was what America was all about. After the museum, the guide said he was going to bring us to the best steakhouse in Washington, which happened to be right across the road. So off we trotted to the best steakhouse in Washington DC, which had five black bouncers outside the door, while inside it was nothing but white faces and thousand-dollar suits. The only non-white person in the place had a brown face, and he was carrying a brush and dustpan and wearing an apron. Hey, I told 9C, Martin Luther King's words never even carried across the street, never mind across the country.

They lapped that story up. Like King, with his reference to his children in the speech, I had made it personal. They had question after question about King, civil rights, segregation and that infamous day in Memphis when King was shot by James Earl Ray.

It was a great class. A wonderful class. Maybe the best I had taught all year.

But there's a thought; a thought that hit me like a kick in the head about a minute after the bell had gone. Best class of the year? Yeah, but it's not like it had much competition.

I've done nothing but criticise 9C. Today, they were brilliant. Why? Because they finally stirred themselves?

Or because I did?

Maybe they're not a boring class. Maybe they've just got a damn boring teacher. Maybe I've induced their coma. Maybe it wasn't just that they had engaged with me today but that I had engaged with them. What was that elation I had felt – the elation of feeling what it was like to be an actual teacher again? Like I used to feel? Maybe I'm the black hole I described 9C as, sucking the life out of everything in my orbit? That's why I was so angry with that agent's rejection, isn't it? It wasn't that she hadn't told me I was 'an urgent, original new voice that must be heard'. It was that she hadn't told me I would soon be an ex-teacher.

'Free at last! Free at last! Thank God Almighty ... free at last!'

Not.

# 8 MAY

Fifth years left today on study leave.

They weren't a bad bunch. I've known a lot worse. I remember one particular cohort the school couldn't wait to be shot of, so eager to see the back of them their date of departure was surreptitiously moved forward. Word got around they were planning something – to wreck a few classrooms, or start a food-fight in the canteen: some 'event' to mark the end of their callow youth and mature passage into adulthood – so the Principal simply announced at an assembly that they were free to go. Off they went, their thunder stolen. At a staff meeting later that day, the Principal received a round of applause, but quickly held up a hand to still this congratulation and tell us: 'Yes, that lot are gone… but nature abhors a vacuum.'

Yes, it does. Each new year group presents its own challenges and all you can hope is that you don't get some class with a psycho mix of personalities. The closest I ever came to that was the 'spitting class', 2D, which I mentioned in an earlier entry, where the worst was Patrick with his crazy aunt. Without question, that was the most difficult class I ever taught. Of course, it goes without saying that I mean 'taught' in the loosest, slackest, most slipshod sense of the word. Mismanaged might be a better word. Well, I mismanaged them right up until their GCSEs, which none of them passed. By that time, a few of them had been expelled, but as the Principal sagely opined, 'nature abhors a vacuum', and a few other head-bangers had joined the class. One of them was Brian. Now, Brian would have given Patrick a run for his money. Thankfully, Patrick was gone by the time Brian showed. With both of them in the same class, I definitely would've been signing on within the week. Anyway, one day I was cursing Brian in and out of hell to a colleague. This colleague had a novel solution to my problem.

'Tell him you're going to let slip that he's a kiddie-fiddler.'

'Excuse me?'

My colleague shrugged. 'You're only telling the truth,' he said.

It seemed that Brian's family had to flee wherever they came from. Brian had been accused of interfering with a little girl and the local righteous brigade were about to show him exactly what they thought of such behaviour i.e. they were going to ventilate his knees. My colleague had got wind of this. It fitted with Brian suddenly appearing on our rolls towards the end of fourth year.

'But he might have been accused in the wrong,' I said to my colleague.

'I don't think so,' said my colleague.

'You told him that?'

My colleague smiled.

Whatever that smile meant, I didn't use that information. I couldn't. With Brian's class, it seemed like the law of the jungle at times, but I wasn't going to stoop that low. I just put up with him. I put my head down and put up with the lot of them. There was one halcyon period when I discovered something they liked – word-searches. If I gave them a word-search, there wasn't a peep for ten minutes or so. For a period of about two months, I taught everything through word-searches. I've never been more inventive. For instance, when we were doing Brian Friel's *Philadelphia, Here I Come!* I would write a character description as the clue: 'Skinflint; a man who finds it impossible to put his feelings into words.' The class would have to identify this as S. B. O' Donnell and then find his name in an elaborate A3-sized word-search I had spent half the night before constructing. I would pinpoint a theme in the play such as 'communication' and they would have to find that in the maze of words. And so on. Then they would create their own word-searches and devise clues, which meant they had to read through the play or my notes. Then I would photocopy their word-searches and divide them up amongst the class. Clever, eh? Not really, because nine times out of ten they made a balls of the spelling on the grid and this produced more fucking and blinding than a call for last orders in a pub in a naval port. Invariably the word-search would be balled up and thrown at its originator (which, I suppose, looking on the bright side, is a step up from spitting on somebody).

All in all, though... Mad!

So they tired of that, just like they tired of everything, until the day they walked down the school avenue for the last time. Before they did, I got a class photograph taken. We posed as if we were a football team, me hunkered down in the front like I was the captain, all of us smiling and cheering – them because they were finishing school, me because I had survived them. I could kid myself that the photograph itself was a kind of success, that we had forged some tenuous kind of bond. And, as I say, they had stopped spitting on one another. As definitions of success go, though, that's a pretty low bar. The odd time we could have a civil conversation – about sports, hobbies, what they were going to do when they left school. At times, there was a sustained lull in their base underhand bastardry. As for work, though – as for the actual job I was being paid to do – it was an absolute dead loss. As I said, they all failed miserably in their exams.

I pinned that photograph up behind my desk. When I got another job, I pinned it up behind my new desk. What was I trying to say? I don't know. I just look at their faces, imagine where they are now. Brian is caught mid-yell, both his arms in the air, his fist clenched. I haven't seen him since he left. Where is he now? In jail? Dead? Married with kids?

All of these children pass through your care. For a brief time, they are central to your existence. Then you forget them. Even the ones who kept you awake at night. Remarkable, but you do. Years later, they'll say hello to you in Tesco or on the street and you won't have the first clue who they are, never mind remember their names. So maybe that's why I still keep that photograph behind my desk. I never want to forget that class. I never want to get nostalgic about that time… or this job.

I write all this because Jessica, a fifth year, knocked on my door before she left. I taught her in first and second year. She said she wanted to speak to me. I followed her out onto the corridor where she gave me a card. 'What's this?' I asked her in surprise. I opened the card and read the message: 'Thanks for fighting so hard for me to be moved up. If you hadn't I would have lost heart.'

'I'm just saying thanks,' she said, and opened her arms for a hug. As I say, I was surprised, and gave her a tentative hug – she'd have got more reaction wrapping her arms around a pole – and wished her good luck. It was true that I had asked for her to be moved up from the middle stream to top stream three years previously. She was a hard worker and deserved it. But her scores across all subjects didn't justify that. I argued that weighting should be given to her good performances in English and Maths and eventually the Head of Year, who was in charge of the decision, saw sense.

Back in class, I thought about pinning her card up beside the group photograph.

One token of success beside one of absolute failure.

But I didn't. I put Jessica's card in my pocket.

That's the way I feel right now.

# 9 MAY

I checked my email at lunchtime and read the following cyber-space chatter from the previous few hours:

11:02 PC sent to Form for refusing to work and being disruptive

11:32 AB has left my room without permission. Just got up and left

11:56 AJ sent to Form. Growling, groaning, rude. Very bizarre and threatening behaviour.

12:45 BC Year 12 sent to form-teacher for refusing to follow simple instructions and then continuing to shout and argue. Wouldn't do anything I asked. I tried to speak to him quietly outside room but his behaviour continued and was distracting the rest of the class. Sorry G_____ [form-teacher].

12:59 AWOL – TD. Just walked out of class. No reason, no explanation. Just left.

Another day, another dollar. But I hope you see the point

of what I mentioned before, about what an ass-ache it can be to be a form-teacher. There you are, discussing the accessibility of Simon Armitage's verse or explaining the difference between 'affective' and 'effective' (which, half the time when I'm going through an exercise, I wish someone would explain to me), and in saunters young Billy with his issues. While in charge of my last form-class, I was teaching first years one Friday afternoon, them hanging on my every fifth or sixth word or so, when one of my 'team', one of my little darlings, balloons in through my door and without so much as a howdy-doody declares one of my esteemed male colleagues to be 'nothin' but a big fat baldy cunt!' Twenty seconds later, the 'big fat baldy cunt' in question appeared. Legs astride, face the colour of a fire extinguisher, the afternoon sun shining on the dome of his skull, my colleague looks at me and jabs a finger at this boy, who had commented on his diet regimen (or lack of one), amongst other things: 'Do *you* know what he called me?' Yes, I did. I looked at my class of cowering first years: we *all* did. Then… I burst out laughing. I swear. I couldn't help myself. It was the end of a long day at the end of a long week and I was tired and this situation just seemed, well, ridiculous. Again, it's this thing about teachers being human. So I laughed. Maybe it was insane laughter, but it was laughter nevertheless, and it was totally unprofessional, and totally not what anyone expected… *and it worked!* In different circumstances, things could have got really ugly, but my colleague, somehow – to his credit – saw the funny side. He started to laugh, then the first years, then the name-caller was laughing too. A few minutes later, after a heartfelt apology in the corridor, my little darling returned to class.

Definitely not one for the textbooks, but humour… well, sometimes it's the only defence against the avalanche of shite coming down the pipes. Sometimes. When it dries up, though – the humour, not the shite (the shite never dries up) – that's when the rot sets in.

I was talking to a senior manager in his mid-fifties this morning who could hardly contain his glee as he told me he had just received confirmation of his redundancy. I was a little taken aback. This guy seemed to live and breathe the school. He was popular with the kids and with the staff and had only just been promoted onto the senior management team. He liked the new Principal, as well, and always had a good word about her and her methods. I asked him what he was going to do with himself in his retirement and he answered, 'Live a bit longer.' He told me the redundancy package was far from what he might have wished, but he had a tough fourth-year class, and the prospect of looking at them for another year and trying to get them through GCSEs… 'Fuck that!' he says. He shrugged. 'I'm done.'

# 15 MAY

As part of the newspaper unit with 8D, we were looking at the Classifieds. I went through what the Classifieds were and set them a homework where they were to write three Classifieds for items they wanted to sell.

Irene wrote:

---

**For Sale: BIG BROTHER**

**Answers to the name Paul.**

**Cute or thinks he is. Big floppy ears.**

**House trained but does have some accidents.**

**Will eat anything.**

**Free to a good home**

---

Not bad, eh? Irene admitted she'd had some help from home. But there was no need to apologise, I told her; that's why it's called homework. I laughed. So did the class. (I loved the 'big floppy ears' and in the ensuing discussion we discovered that Irene's big brother did indeed have such ears.)

Jill wrote this:

---

**Black ass for Sale**

**Like new**

**£90 o.n.o.**

---

The class laughed at this too. I had a number of questions and was wondering if social services should become involved, but Jill protested that she hadn't written 'ass', she had written '95s' ('It's the way I do my nines – Gawd sake!'), which I'm told are a type of shoe. I cautioned Jill to watch her handwriting.

Finally, Ethan, who – not for the first time – had confused the whole exercise and instead of writing a 'For sale' Classified had written a 'Wanted' one. Still, his work is worth reprinting:

---

**Wanted**

**English teacher**

**Patients needed**

**headache tablets included**

**Shouting not aloud.**

---

Lovely.

# 16 MAY

I was explaining how to write a newspaper report to 8D. I was explaining it very slowly and very carefully because I know they will struggle with it. Most classes struggle with it. A good reason for this is that they don't read newspapers. Why do a newspaper unit, then? Because I wanted them to see what was in a newspaper. Maybe something would catch their interest. Also, writing a newspaper report is a good discipline where they must answer the five key questions: Who? What? Where? When? and Why? It forces them out of their comfort zone, pushes them to write in third-person objective and is also useful in terms of how it requires them to use quotations and set them out properly when they write up eyewitness statements.

All in all, nourishment for the brain.

But, as I say, they can find it difficult to get their heads around. So, there I was, explaining that a newspaper report tells the same story three times: first, with the headline; second, in the opening paragraphs as it answers the five key questions; third, in the main body of the report, which expands on the answers to the key questions, mostly through

background information and eyewitness statements. Extolling the importance of the Fourth Estate, and feeling all
Woodward and Bernstein-y, I drew a triangle on the board
to illustrate the tripartite nature of a news report.

To repeat – and I was doing a lot of repeating – I was
taking baby steps, and I needed 8D's full focus and concentration, and it was going well... when, all of a sudden, totally
out of the blue, Orinoco shot out of his seat and started pat-
ting his pockets. Yes, that's right – Orinoco, named not after
the lazy and greedy Womble – how the hell would these
kids have heard of the Wombles? – but because when asked
to name the longest river in South America in Geography
class, he had answered that it was the Orinoco. Even though
it was the wrong answer, I was astonished to learn that this
lad had heard of the Orinoco River and so was everyone else
within earshot; hence, Orinoco (that's how dangerous a little
knowledge can be in a classroom. Forevermore, I will think
of Orinoco whenever I hear that idiom repeated).

Anyway, back to the action. And action it was. In a heart-
beat, Orinoco appeared overcome with an absolute panic.
I mean, he couldn't have been in any more of a flap if his
trousers had been on fire.

'David?' Yes, his real name, although the syllable 'Or-'
might have slipped from my lips before I caught myself.

He was so shaken he didn't even seem to hear me. By
now he was down on his knees and looking under the table.
He hauled his schoolbag onto his desk and began rifling
through it.

'Have you lost your phone?' I asked him.

He looked at me blankly and patted his pockets again and then looked wildly around.

'*David!*' I commanded.

This seemed to call him back to reality.

'What?' I asked him.

His lips quivered. He seriously looked on the point of tears, barely able to speak. He might have been one of those people you read about who suddenly receive a shock or a jolt, as if from nowhere, and are filled with a telepathic dread that a loved one in some distant place has suffered a terrible injury. Had Orinoco received a message of such primal, dreadful urgency that it shattered all the laws of the physical universe? That would certainly explain the last minute or so.

'What, David?' I asked again.

He looked round at his classmates. I couldn't decide whether that look was wounded or vengeful. 'Somebody...' he said.

'Somebody what?'

He was finally able to gather his senses enough to muster a sentence.

'*Somebody stole my Chupa Chups!*'

The class erupted.

I needed a moment. 'Your what?'

'My Chupa Chups!' he wailed, his mouth hanging like a bucket.

I told him to leave the room and I followed him out. This for two reasons: one, so I could tell the class that I wanted those whatever-the-fuck-they-were sitting on Orinoco's desk by the time I returned or else I was keeping everybody over lunch; two, I wanted to tear a strip out of him.

There he was in the corridor, the innocent victim of a capital offence, arms tightly folded, his expression sullen and defiant. I asked him what the hell he thought he was playing at.

'Somebody stole my Chupa Chups,' he says, his lips quivering again.

'I don't give a damn. I'm trying to teach a lesson here and you're behaving like a two-year-old!'

'They're mine,' he says, while putting his head down and folding his arms even tighter.

After a few more denunciations of this preschool whining, I finished with: 'Wise up!'

We went back into the room. The Chupa Chups, a packet of lollipops, were sitting on his desk. He gathered them up without a look at anybody and put them in his pocket. Scowling, he hunched down in his seat. I had to settle the class *again*, threaten them with lunch detention *again*. I went back to the board and began *again*. 'Now, newspaper reports; as I was saying...'

'They've took some of them!'

Orinoco was brandishing the packet of Chupa Chups – I mean, what the fuck? Why do I have to write sentences like this? – like peace in our time. To be clear, this wasn't anarchic humour, or any devious attempt to disrupt the lesson or play silly buggers on his part. No, this was totally serious; this was vindication, this was Exhibit A, this was 'somebody's had my lovely sweeties that my lovely mommy bought me'.

'*They took some of them!*'

'Get out!' I roared.

I sent him to the Year Head. If I hadn't, those lollipops would've become suppositories.

Writing this about Orinoco, I found it impossible not to contrast him with the foreign students in 10P earlier in the morning. The class were working on their Shakespeare projects and the four foreign girls were flying ahead. Two of them are Romanian and the other two are Portuguese. Their English is absolutely basic but they weren't letting that stop them. I was hesitant about setting them the project, but they were enjoying cutting and pasting and creating a document and working on it to make it look good, even if they didn't understand a lot of its substance.

Then again, the English-speaking students didn't understand a lot of its substance. Laura had written a page of famous Shakespeare quotes. I didn't recognise one of them, though: 'You know you're in love when you can't fall asleep because reality is finally better than your dreams.'

I Googled this myself. It was Dr Seuss.

'Isn't he in Shakespeare?' says Laura.

Anyhow, the foreign students had run up against a problem. A key part of the project was to read one of the condensed Shakespeare texts and write a summary. This wasn't going to happen. What to do? They puzzled over the word 'summary'. We Googled it in Romanian and Portuguese and found 'rezumat' and 'resumo'. OK, now they could find a rezumat or resumo in Romanian or Portuguese of a Shakespeare play and then try to translate it into English. First, they had to pick a play. I explained to them about tragedy ('sad'), romance ('love') and comedy (they knew what that was already). I ignored 'historical' (what – tell them these were set in 'the past' / 'long ago'?). The Romanian girls settled on romance and *Romeo and Juliet*; the Portuguese went for tragedy and *King Lear*. Does that say anything about national character?

For a full hour they worked solidly on this with not one complaint. Yes, plenty of questions, but no grumbling, no 'What is this "thee" shit?' (This from Tracy).

As I say, I can't help making the comparison: comparing, say, their seriousness about this work and Orinoco's seriousness about his Chupa Chups.

Am I drawing some Brexitan analogy?

Fuck it, I am.

These Romanian and Portuguese girls are industrious, determined and well-mannered despite, or because of, the seismic upheaval in their lives. Won't our society benefit from the presence and influence of such people?

What about Orinoco and his ilk? What will they bring to the party? I'm not arguing Orinoco is representative in any way – Christ, I hope not. But I bet if he was a few years older, and had the vote, he'd be perfect bait for anyone who told him that the reason he hadn't got a job or his life wasn't what it should be was because of all those foreigners. Provided he could lever himself out of bed, I bet he'd vote for a party led by someone who looked like Mr Toad. Am I saying that all Brexiteers are spoilt brats? No, I am certainly not. However, I'll wager they get the spoilt brat vote.

Then again, I could be all wrong about Orinoco. Maybe he will wise up. I doubt it, but it's possible. (Didn't even Charlie Sheen recognise he was a complete dick?) It's not beyond the realm of possibility that maybe Orinoco will wake up to himself. Maybe one day he'll prove useful to someone other than his mother.

And share his Chupa Chups.

# 20 MAY

I had to talk to a teacher today about his class discipline. Not that his discipline was lacking, it was that he was trying out a new approach. This approach consisted of significantly lowering his voice. 'Whispering Bob Harris' – as he'd now been dubbed – told me about it a month or so before and said it was working, that the pupils had to remain perfectly quiet in order to hear him. He thought he was onto something. Now, when he did raise his voice, it had the desired effect as well. So far, so good, except in the meantime a class I was covering had him for a double after me. The bell went. Cue general grumbling. I asked what was up. The reason for such discontent when it came to Whispering Bob? They couldn't hear him. 'He just mumbles,' said one girl. 'I haven't a clue what he's on about.'

Classroom management, discipline; mine's not the best but, generally, for the most part, I keep a lid on things. Yet I will freely admit I lack that conviction that marks out the best classroom managers, the proper disciplinarians.

And that's the word…

*Conviction!*

Lowering your voice…

Not smiling till Christmas…

Fully preparing your lessons…

Or even being an unhinged and truly frightening bastard (I've been taught by a few of those).

They all may help, but nothing creates good discipline like having conviction, like believing totally in the job you're doing, or at least giving the impression that you believe in it. At the same time, I don't think you can truly fake that. You'll be found out at some point. I suppose it's the same in any profession. The best are those who say what they mean and mean what they say. In teaching, it's especially important. Children can smell a rat – a jobsworth – a mile off.

I remember my teacher training and the lectures on classroom management. These lectures were always the best-attended. There we would be, a hundred of us prospective pedagogues, bricking it at the thought of all the acne and hormones we would shortly be standing in front of, our pens hovering, our ears cocked, waiting, begging, praying to be told the secret. Yet all we had to do was think back to the best teachers we had. What marked them out? What distinguished them? What was their secret? Answer: they cared. They gave a damn. They made us feel that our wellbeing and happiness and success meant something to them.

Basically, there is no secret. How many books or papers or theses have been written on the subject? I'm sure they would stretch to the moon.

But it just means loving the job. Or liking it, at least.
I'm telling you.
It's that easy.
And that hard.

# 23 MAY

'That's what they said at Auschwitz.'

It was break-time and I was having to clear the pupils off the far pitch. They aren't allowed on the far pitch at break. At lunch, they are, but at break they're not. I don't know the rationale except since it takes them two minutes or so to walk to the far pitch from the exit doors, and the same to walk back, that's a lot of their break used up. It can also mean they might be late for the class directly after break. Of the former, so what? Walking will do them good, won't it? Of the latter, there's a three-minute bell that goes off after the end of break to signal the corridors should be clear. So what's the problem?

To repeat, I don't know why they're not allowed on the far pitch.

Anyway, fuck it, I was to clear them off.

As usual, this was met with some protest. 'But we're allowed here at lunchtime!' says Simon. 'So why are we not allowed at break?'

'I don't know,' I says. 'I suppose it takes you lot too long to get back into class after the bell goes if you're down here.'

'But there's the other bell,' says Aaron. 'It's no sweat. We've got three minutes.'

Didn't I say about that three-minute bell?

'Look, would you just do what you're told?' I says. 'You're not allowed down here. That's all there is to it. I don't make the rules.'

'You're just following orders,' says Aaron.

'That's right.'

That's when Aaron made his Auschwitz crack.

I pretended great offence. 'What the hell kind of thing is that to say?'

Aaron stood his ground. 'But it is,' he says. 'Yous are always saying all this stuff about thinking for yourselves.' Aaron had been at the Spectrum meeting I attended. He had a bit about him. And, of course, he was absolutely 100 per cent correct.

Still, I had a zinger for him. 'My great-grandfather died at Auschwitz,' I told him.

He grunted a laugh. 'Aye, right!' he says. But I was wearing my really serious face. An undertaker couldn't have looked more dismal. 'Really?' he says.

'Aye, he fell out of a watch-tower.'

'Huh?' says Aaron. Then his head rocked back like he'd been jabbed on the nose. 'You can't say something like that.'

At least he got the joke, if joke it might be called. But I wasn't finished. I decided to persevere. 'Why not? It's true.'

'Aye, right!' he repeated. 'Your great-granda was a Nazi?'

'Bewegen!' I told him.

'What?' he says.

'It's "move" in German,' I said.

He looked at me funny.

'Schnell, schweinehund!' I cried. 'Schnell, schnell!'

I don't know, I was in that kind of mood today. Like when I walked in after break and brought 8D down to the computer room. They were to design a newspaper front page on Microsoft Publisher. Unsurprisingly, I had to teach them how to use the programme. At one point, Cathy put her hand up and asked me how to move down the page. She didn't know how to use the return button. I mean, what the feck were these kids actually doing in primary school? Jason, whose mom put in the complaint about him not getting enough homework, put his hand up. I wandered over to him.

'How am I supposed to write on this?' he says.

I looked at his monitor. Somehow he had reduced the zoom to 15 per cent and he was looking at a page the size of a postage stamp.

'It's too small,' he practically wailed. 'This is stupid!'

Without comment, I went to adjust the zoom and bring the page up to normal size. Then I hesitated. Sometimes you just feel like being a bollix. 'It *is* stupid,' I says. 'See if you can write on it anyway.'

'But it's too small!'

'Just see what you can do, Jason,' I told him. 'For me.'

So I left Jason to gnash his teeth and get more and more angry as he tried to decipher the minuscule words he was writing. If he had been looking at them through a compound microscope he would have struggled. Meanwhile, I would tut and shake my head and make generally sympathetic noises each time I came back over to where he was sitting. 'I don't know,' I would say. 'I've never seen that before.'

'It's stupid!'

He *was* wailing now.

'What's that you've written?'

'*I can't see it!*'

I tutted some more. Shook my head some more. 'I can't understand it.' I let this go on for twenty minutes before I put the child out of his misery and adjusted the zoom.

Like Aaron, Jason didn't see the funny side.

'You knew that the whole time!' he exploded. 'That's not right.'

No, it wasn't.

Like when Vicky turned up in class today. I haven't seen her in about a month. She's a very pretty girl and, like some very pretty girls, she thinks her looks are all she needs, which makes her terribly ugly. I set some work down in front of her. She turned up her little pointy nose. She's on report so I asked for her report card and wrote 'Excellent work' on it.

'But I haven't done any,' she says.

'And you won't, Vicky, just like you never do,' I says. 'So I'm writing that so that I don't bother you and you don't bother me. OK?'

'OK,' she shrugs.

There was a general air of insouciance about me today. That's couldn't-give-a-fuckery, for those who don't know. I did my job, I taught my classes, but… it's like when I was driving to work this morning. Steve Harley's 'Make Me Smile' was playing on the radio. It's one of my favourites and I was really enjoying it with the sound up full blast. Christ, but this was a good start to the day. Then there's that dead stop before Jim Cregan's glorious acoustic guitar solo. To my mind, it's one of the greatest solos in pop history. And what happened? The DJ, some absolute fuckwit, starts talking over the solo. In fact, he talked over the rest of the song.

But to talk over that piece of genius guitar playing…!

Everything today felt like those plums that the poet William Carlos Williams took out of the icebox that his lover was saving for breakfast before he ate them instead in an act of spite.

Writing this down, I think I might be cracking up.

# 30 MAY

I've sat down to write a diary entry these last three nights. My fingers hover on the keyboard, but there's nothing to report except that it's been raining all week. Nearly June and it looks like November outside my window (why the hell would anyone want to fight and die for this miserable country?).

Nothing to report today, either. Cathal asked me if Shakespeare wrote *The Lion King*. That got a laugh from the rest of the class (even from Nina; she of the black South African Shakespeare who definitely wasn't Michael Jackson). But Cathal had just mis-read something because *The Lion King* was supposedly based on Hamlet. I told the class this to save Cathal's blushes. (I don't know, but when I saw *The Lion King*, *Hamlet* didn't immediately spring to mind. Yes, Uncle Scar kills Simba's father, but that's about it. There's no play within a play: Simba's girlfriend, Nala, doesn't kill herself. If Timon and Pumbaa are Rosencrantz and Guildenstern, I'm a warthog's uncle. Based on *Hamlet* my arse!)

Later, I was back in the computer suite with 8D. I showed

them a front page of the *Belfast Telegraph* and told them that after drawing up the newspaper report they'd written the week before, they were now to use it as the lead story on a front page designed like the *Telegraph*'s front page, inserting adverts, referencing inside stories, finding an eye-catching photo somewhere on the internet that would serve the story they had written. The whole time, I was pointing to the *Telegraph*. 'It has to look something like this. You understand? That's a full two periods' work. I don't want to hear "I'm finished" ten minutes in.'

And ten minutes in?

Then I pull Chantelle for being out of her seat. I speak to her in the corridor. Chantelle has turned into a right little madam lately: defiant, rude, lazy.

'Why were you out of your seat?'

'Needed some help,' says Chantelle. If she had answered, 'Go fuck yourself,' there would have been no discernible difference in tone or pronunciation.

'What do you do when you need help?'

'Ask.'

'Ask who?'

'Somebody.'

'Who's paid to provide help in such circumstances?'

'Wha?'

'Who are you supposed to ask for help?'

'A friend.'

'No, that's *Who Wants to Be a Millionaire?*'

'Wha?'

'You do know that you sound like a duck with a Northern Irish accent?'

'Wha?'

'Wouldn't you agree that I'm the person you're supposed to ask for help? Me, your teacher?'

'Suppose.'

'And instead of getting out of our seat, what do we do?'

'Ask for help.'

'How do we ask for help?

'Just ask for it.'

'What do we do first? It's on the end of your arm there.'

'My hand?'

'What do you do with it?'

'Put it up.'

'Put it up what?'

I admit I phrased that last question badly, but to phrase it any way other than badly would've meant I was thinking about what I was saying. I hadn't thought about what I was saying for a full week now (and, yes, some people would say never).

'Wha?'

'You put your hand up and you say, "Excuse me…?" There should be a wee word on the end of that "excuse me" – the title you address me by.'

'Wha?'

I felt like throwing her some bread. Instead, I said, 'It begins with an "s", it ends with an "r", and it's got three letters which means the remaining, middle letter, situated as it is between two consonants, must be a vowel.'

I knew these last few clauses would only confuse Chantelle but she got there in the end: 'Sir?'

'Congratulations. Now, let's take it from the beginning...'

After lunch, 9C were giving their speeches. Twelve-year-old Martin had written a speech on drugs. I'll spare you his opening remarks. Verbatim, here's his peroration:

Cocaine can kill you if you take too much. That's why you have to be careful with cocaine. There are some types of drugs in the world like that. Now I get on to heroin. I do not know much about heroin. I only know you put it in your arm through a needle and it can kill you. So don't take heroin. The next drug is ecstasy. I do not know what it does to you because I have not taken it. It comes in a tablet form. The next one is Pikes. Some people have not heard of it since it is only found on the area of my estate. It is a type of drug which gets you high and hyper-excited and gives you loads of confidence. The next one is Bines on my estate. It comes in tablet form. You can eat it, crush it up and sniff it. It gets you high. Those are all the drugs I know. Tell me if you know any more.

Tell *me* if you know any more!

I wrote at the start of this entry that there was nothing to report today. There isn't. For a change, I'm not being sarcastic.

Same shit, different day, and I quit laughing a long time ago.

# 3 JUNE

Patricia, Una, Geraldine and Shauna haven't finished their Shakespeare projects yet. The rest of the class are finished but these four girls are only halfway through. Each one of them is a concern for one reason or another.

1. Patricia. I think she's bipolar. Her attendance is pretty ropey but, when present, she's either glum and stone-quiet or full of beans and mildly flirtatious. Today, she's all smiles. She asks me if I'm married and what I do at the weekends. I tell her to try and get a shift on with the project then curse myself for cutting her off. Basically, the project doesn't matter; Patricia doesn't give two damns about it and neither do I, if I'm honest. She's in a good mood and I should be responding to that and playing along.

2. Geraldine. She's become more withdrawn over the past month or so. She was always quiet but now there's hardly a word. It's like she's in a daze. If she was on some kind of tranquilliser, I wouldn't be surprised. There was the *Stone*

*Cold* essay previously where her first effort really let her down. We tidied that up, but maybe that initial draft was a harbinger. Something's bothering her.

3. Una. Una comes in every week with a different hairstyle and a lot of the time it's a dye-job. To boot, she's always plastered in tan and when I say plastered, I mean like a drunk plasterer has applied it, skimming some parts and laying it on thick in others. She has a few spots – nothing major, nothing to wet the bed about – but covered in this bad tan it's like a bar of Fruit & Nut has exploded in her face. I feel a pity for a girl who must be so unhappy with her natural looks.

4. Shauna. She's just scatty, as my granny would have said. She's all over the place, so easily distracted, but always good-natured, always pleasant. I've never seen her in a mood. Then again, maybe she should be in more of a mood sometimes. The others tease her and bully her a little and she just laughs it off. It's nothing really serious, no one's bouncing on her head. Yet I'd love to hear her tell someone to fuck off, and stand up for herself, just the once at least. It would give me some heart that she isn't going to be walked over all her life.

If I was a parent of any of these girls, I would worry about them. I would worry about them a lot. Breaking it right down, it's a problem of confidence. None of these girls have any confidence in themselves. One wrong word can shatter their day. Like I was saying with Patricia: I should have humoured her. I'm making a leap here, and I hope I'm wrong, but I would wager these young women are easy prey for the first person who shows so much as a passing interest in them. Odds are, they will be pregnant by their late teens. A baby will give them status (in their own heads, at least) and some foothold in this thing called life. Yet it will be a slippery foothold. Slippery because there is no locus of control. They will not be in control: the husband or partner will be in control, the baby will be in control and, worst-case scenario, social agencies will be in control. These girls will have no personal resources to fall back on, no sense of accomplishment or achievement or inner belief. In such circumstances, life can become very hard very quickly. And in so many years' time, that baby might be in these very seats, trying to catch up on their Shakespeare project, with somebody else worried about them. The Circle of Life but with fuck all resemblance to *The Lion King* (or *Hamlet*).

As I say, I hope I'm wrong, but I've seen it too many times.

So I'm chivvying them along to get some more work done. Hey, a little Shakespeare is all they need, right? Meanwhile, the rest of the class are in the computer suite as well. Since they've finished their projects and exams are next week, I tell them to use the computers for revision: they can look up a topic they're struggling with in Maths or History or Geography or whatever. It's last periods and none of them are up for it – they'd rather play games or look at images of their favourite singers – but they go through the motions. It's a nudge-nudge-wink-wink, if they don't bother me, I won't bother them situation: so long as nobody decides to throw a chair across the room, they can pretty much sit and talk to one another.

Which is pretty much what they do. Except Katrina wasn't talking, she was listening, to the breathless girls either side of her, Laura and Tracy. Nosey bastard that I am, I couldn't help straining an ear as Laura and Tracy explained to Katrina how she got into a fight the previous Friday night. It seems that Katrina needed this explained to her because she had absolutely no recollection as a result of drinking half a litre of vodka. Of this imbibement, there didn't seem to be any mixer involved, or debonaire rattle of ice cubes in a tumbler of Waterford Crystal; no, it was straight from the neck. 'You were so out of it, Katrina babes!' Laura trilled. Tracy concurred and commented that it was just like the previous two weekends when Katrina had got involved in fights. Katrina seemed to have won the fights hands down. So that was all right then.

Katrina is thirteen!

Is it old-fashioned of me to be shocked at this? I don't think it is. This fighting supposedly took place at 'the underpass'. I've heard of this underpass; stories of kids gathering in this pedestrian tunnel under the motorway on Friday and Saturday nights. Hundreds of underage kids. Urban legend has it that parents drop them off with carry-outs.

The conversation continues as Laura and Tracy talk about some other girl called Linda.

'Aw, she's a mouth!' says Laura.

'She can't hold her drink,' says Tracy.

I had to step in here. 'Excuse me?' I says. 'Hold her drink?'

Tracy reddens when she realises I've been eavesdropping. 'But she can't,' she says weakly.

'And you can?'

'I don't drink,' says Tracy. 'I just go for the craic, sir.'

I look at Katrina. 'Sounds like a lot of craic.'

Katrina says nothing.

'All these people who come in here talking about the dangers of drink and drugs, and what it can do to your bodies at your age,' I continue. 'Are you paying any attention at all?' I never got any of these talks when I was at school, but I knew... Ah, forget it, I'm a fuckin' hypocrite! I know I am. Still, I wasn't blind drunk and fighting in an underpass at age thirteen (I was in my twenties. I think. I can't really remember).

'I don't do drink or drugs!' says Tracy, getting stroppy now.

The rest of the class are listening. Dermot pipes up: 'Ah now, you like your wee Bacardi Breezer alcopops, Trace.'

Tracy rounds on him. 'Sure, that's not drinking, ya slabber, ya!'

Should I report this? Should I ring the contact number for Katrina and speak to whoever's supposed to be looking after her? They might tell me I'm telling lies, or that Laura and Tracy are telling lies. Conversely, they might appreciate the call. Then again, they must be in some way suspicious that she's drinking. Jesus, are they blind? One thing they can't tell me, though, is that it's none of my business. How can I hope to impose any discipline on Katrina in a classroom situation when no discipline seems to exist at home? (Suffice to say that, if a parent was called in for a meeting about Katrina, the first thing they'd have to say was that she didn't seem to get any homework.)

Anyhow – any-fucking-how! – humming 'What Kind of Fool Am I' and feeling like I'm a hundred and ten, I retire from the fray and return to the four girls I was expressing worry about.

Ha!

Patricia and Una were trying to find examples of Shakespearian sonnets. Shauna was searching for a movie adaptation of *Romeo and Juliet*. Meanwhile, Geraldine was looking at the question, 'Why is Shakespeare still relevant today?' She doesn't know what this means. I sit down beside her, and start on about *Twelfth Night* and how it was the first Shakespeare I ever read. I tell her I'd heard about this writer who was supposed to be very difficult to understand but who wasn't really all that difficult. I told her I'd read the play at about her age and loved it. I told her about it being the middle of the Troubles, and the news every day was frightening, but *Twelfth Night* lifted me out of all that and gave me something to smile about. I told her about bunking off school to go home and watch it. She laughed at this. I hadn't seen her laugh in a while. I asked her if she was OK, said that she had been very quiet lately. She just shrugged; said she was OK. I continued about *Twelfth Night* and told her that when I was feeling down or out of sorts, I sometimes went back to the play and read parts from it, and it often cheered me up – all that sun and happiness and love and laughter and friendship.

'Sounds good,' she said.

'Yeah,' I told her. 'Maybe you'd like to take a look at it?'

She snorts. '*Me, Shakespeare!* I wouldn't get it, sir.'

She's probably right. What am I saying? She's undoubtedly right. Geraldine struggled with *Stone Cold*. Still, didn't the uneducated come in their droves to the Globe Theatre? Wasn't Shakespeare the Spielberg of his day?

'Couldn't hurt to try, Geraldine?' I suggest.

Now, if I was making this all up, or this was a shit movie and I was Robin Williams – even though he's dead – Geraldine would shrug and say something like, 'I suppose'. Then, when I was feeling rock-bottom a few weeks later, staring out my classroom window and contemplating what a dog's dinner I'd made of my life or somebody else's, a jubilant cry would sound behind me: 'If music be the food of love, play on!' Desperate with hope, I would turn and there would be a beaming Geraldine poised in the doorway, a copy of *Twelfth Night* clutched to her bosom, the light of adoration shining in her eyes (adoration for me, of course, not Shakespeare).

Instead, since I am not making this up, and since this is not a really terrible movie, and because there are no arcs here, only troughs, what happens? Geraldine seems to consider what I have just said before she looks at the question again. She says it out loud. 'Why is Shakespeare still...' She pauses over 'relevant' then asks me, 'How do you say that word again?'

# 7 JUNE

8D are finishing off their newspaper front pages. Louis has finished. I tell him to use this time to revise on the computer, same as I did with 10P. This time, though, I mean it. I tell Louis I don't want to hear a word out of him otherwise I'm keeping him behind at lunch. He tells me he can't do lunch detention. I ask why not. He says that another teacher has given him lunch detention. 'What for?' I ask. 'I told him to "chill his beans",' he says.

Emily is spinning round in her seat. I tell her to stop. 'Why?' she says. I tell her to log off the computer and go over to the benches at the other side of the room. Grumbling and groaning, she does so. I then tell her to write me a page entitled 'Why answering back is a bad idea'.

'Why?' she says.

I tell her to write me two pages.

Meanwhile, Chantelle hasn't even logged on to her computer. I ask why not. 'I'm near finished,' she says. I forgo punching holes in this logic and tell her to get a move on. Beside Chantelle, Chloe asks me if she can go to the toilet.

She then says: 'But I might be a really long time, because sometimes it takes a really long time to come out.' She says this quite loudly and unabashedly, but nobody comments. I tell her to take as long as her colon needs.

Just down from her, Kyle has his hand up. I ask him what's wrong. He tells me he can't remember his password. I ask him how the hell he can't remember it when he's been using it for the past two weeks. He shrugs and says it isn't working. I tell him to keep on trying. Then Thomas has his hand up. He points to a correction I had made in his hand-written newspaper report. I had changed his spelling of 'leftenant' to 'lieutenant'. Thomas looks bewildered. Saying that, Thomas often looks bewildered. But he's adamant he has spelt the word correctly. 'Fine,' I tell him, 'fill your boots, Thomas.'

Robert is flopped back in his seat, staring at the ceiling, his arms hanging limp. It's like his throat has been cut. I ask him the problem. He manages to lift a hand to gesture at the monitor and then drops the hand again as if it's all too much. It seems he is finished (with the newspaper report, not ex-istentially). I pick up the *Telegraph* front page of which his work is meant to be a simulacrum. I have to be positive in this job, so I comment that the *Telegraph* page and Robert's effort are both rectangular in outline. After that, I'm strug-gling. Robert doesn't seem too bothered, though. I ask him if he's tired. He nods weakly. I tell him to have a little nap. Does he want a blanket to put over him? He shakes his head – again, very weakly. I tell the class to keep it down, that Robert needs forty winks. He seems to get it now: that I mightn't be 100 per cent serious. I tell him to sit up straight and do a proper bloody headline at the top of his story.

Shannon now has her hand up. She says she's finished, and wants to know if she can print her page. The work looks decent except for a picture of the Queen underneath the headline 'This Woman Saw A ghost'. I had told the class to write a few smaller front-page 'filler' stories. Shannon's filler reads, 'The Queen seen a ghost last night, She said it was green and she could see through it.'

'Don't you think that would be the *headline* story, Shannon?' I asked. 'I mean, the Queen of England seeing a ghost! Wouldn't that have the big headline?'

Shannon just looks at me.

'And the headline itself – wouldn't it be "Queen Sees a Ghost"?'

Shannon shrugs.

'Print it up,' I tell her. Life is really too short.

I check on Emily, who had to write the pages about answering back. She has written:

on a bright day we were at school and the teachers were all being moody which made the students very angry and my best mate called Susie. Got shouted at for taking to me so she said she wasn't talking and the teacher sent her out he started to ask me questions and I told him its none of his bussniess and he sent me out. Sir came out with a really red face he was fuming angry he started to point he's fingers in our face me and my best friend looked at

each other and laughed at him which got us in more trouble but being hoesnt none of us care like its really not the
end of the world so you'll be sweet in the morning

'It's very *Finnegans Wake*, isn't it, Emily?'

'Wha?' she says.

'I think you might have something here,' I tell her. Then I
write out the first sentence of *Finnegans Wake* at the bottom of
her page: 'riverrun, past Eve and Adam's, from swerve of shore
to bend of bay, brings us by a commodious vicus of recircula-
tion back to Howth Castle and Environs'. (Just in case you're impressed by this, it's the only line I know from that conundrum
of a novel. I used to be stock-full of lines and passages – see
below. Girls would be impressed by my intelligence and sen-
sitivity. Not as impressed as they were by big muscles, though,
and similarly oversized dicks and cars and bank balances.)

Emily looks at the Joyce like I've spat on the page.

'You see,' I tell her. 'Your work is Joycean, Emily. You go
home and tell your mom and dad—'

'I live with my granny.'

'That's nice.' I continue unconcerned. 'Well, you tell your
old gran that.'

'She's not really old. She's only forty-two.'

I do some mental calculations, then stop. It's too depressing. I go on. 'You tell her you're a Joycean and you won't hear
a word said against the great man. Bloomsday's just around
the corner; I suppose you'll be making the annual pilgrim-
age down to Dublin?'

'Dublin, wha? What man? I don't know what you're on about,' Emily responds, her expression fixed in the scowl that is so constant it's like a logo branded on her face.

'You're too modest,' I tell her while turning to the class and raising my hands above my head in pumping fists. 'Write on, Emily, write on. Give me excess of it that, surfeiting, the appetite may sicken and so die!'

I am going mad, I tell you.

I imagine Lear staggering and howling in the midst of the storm; this old man whose eyes are open for the first time. Then I say the lines. I mean, I say them out loud to the class, totally out of nowhere:

> Poor naked wretches, whereso'er you are,
> That bide the pelting of this pitiless storm,
> How shall your houseless heads and unfed sides,
> Your looped and windowed raggedness, defend you
> From seasons such as these? Oh, I have ta'en
> Too little care of this! Take physic, pomp.
> Expose thyself to feel what wretches feel
> That thou mayst shake the superflux to them
> And show the heavens more just.

I believe these are the most moving lines in the history of literature. I believe that if Shakespeare had only written these lines and nothing else, he would still deserve to be remembered. So I finish, all passion spent... and for the first time this year, 8D are totally silent, looking at me like I'm drunk; like this is a movie moment.

Except they're not, and they aren't, and it isn't.

Instead... it's like they haven't heard a word.

Chloe comes back from the toilets. Chantelle asks her if she went. Chloe shakes her head mournfully, and tells Chantelle and everyone else: 'I still can't go!' Again, remarkably, nobody comments. Nobody so much as smiles, never mind sniggers.

I look round at these strange, alien beings with their strange, alien ways.

You ever feel you've wasted your life?

Or maybe I should just 'chill my beans', as Louis would no doubt tell me.

# 10 JUNE

'I'm leaving.'

'Really?'

'On Wednesday.'

This from Enda. I'd asked him how he was getting on. I'd spoken to his mother on the phone a few weeks back, his work having dipped in the last two assessments.

'Bit sudden,' I said. With only a few weeks left of term, it was a strange time to leave and begin a new school. Or maybe he would take an extended summer holiday and begin the new school in September. Knowing Enda, that made more sense.

'Where are you going?' I said, meaning which school.

'Magaluf,' he says.

I presumed this wasn't Magaluf High.

I regrouped. 'What about your exams?'

'Aw, I'm rippin'!' he says with a smile.

I smiled back. I doubted the Principal would see the humour, though. Then again, neither did I (my smile was rather thin). In our phone conversation previously, after commenting that Enda didn't seem to get enough home-work, his mother had assured me that I was going to see a new and improved Enda. Silly me; I hadn't realised that 'new and improved' meant he was getting a tan.

But it's a common problem, parents taking advantage of cut-price holidays in exam season and jetting off. It shouldn't be allowed. Any parent who indulges in it should find a letter waiting for them when they get home to say they should find another school for their loved one. But with schools so strapped for cash, they need every pupil on their roll. So that letter won't be written and the likes of Enda will continue on our roll. And he will fail his GCSE exams and bring our percentages down. That is written in the stars. He is already struggling, and with this level of home support, he will give up the struggle. Of that, I am certain. You can take that to the bank.

For an undersubscribed school like ours, the bottom line is putting as many bums on seats as possible, no matter how shitty those bums, if you'll forgive the metaphor. That means we are loath to expel, which means that intolerable behaviour can become tolerable. It also means we will accept anyone who applies to the school. That also means accepting three or four pupils during the year who have been expelled from other schools. This in itself is intolerable. These expelled pupils are different from convicted felons, who will often maintain their innocence to their dying day. The exact opposite, in fact – these 'villains' will loudly proclaim their bastardry and often continue it, adding their noxious influence to an already heady brew. Accepting this rabble onto our rolls, it's like what they say about marrying for money: that you earn every penny. (That's true, too; witness Melania Trump and her death's-head smile: watch real close when her husband takes her hand, and that rictus grin falters for just a beat, and a psychotic little tic starts to pulse at the top of her cheek, just under her left eye.)

But what can our school do?

An interesting fact came to light in the inspection report which has just been released. Overall, the report made grim reading. Essentially, stripping away all the bullshit, schools are judged according to the percentage of pupils who have attained five or more GCSEs or equivalent at grades A* to C. Our percentage was below the national average. The inspectors concluded that 'outcomes in public examinations … require improvement'. Yet the Vice-Principal had done his sums as well. He presented the inspectors with our percentage of grades A* to C according to those pupils who had been with us for five years, from Year 8 through to GCSE – that is, he excluded the blow-ins. Lo and behold: in these new figures, our percentage was above the national average. In other words, we're doing a good job. A great job, I would argue, considering our circumstances.

The inspectors didn't include this in the report.

Didn't I tell you about them?

So we're in a Catch-22. We are an undersubscribed school because of our exam results (even though our results are good according to the unofficial statistics) and because we are undersubscribed we must take in expelled pupils from other schools (while trying our damndest not to get rid of present pupils who, five or ten years ago, would have been told to sling their hooks), which further depresses our results (not to mention our staff), which means we are further undersubscribed, which means... ah, you get the gist.

Ever-decreasing circles, like water swirling down a drain. Except it's not water – it's us.

That's the reality of our situation; the reality that never makes it into the statistics.

And that's why Enda can quite openly tell me he's going on holiday to Magaluf, and fuck his exams. In an oversubscribed school, this wouldn't be allowed to happen. Or he would keep his mouth shut, or tell a few little white lies, at least. ('How'd you get that tan, Enda?' 'Oh, we were up at Portrush at the weekend, and it was real sunny for about twenty minutes and I slapped some cooking oil on myself...')

Talking of porky pies, I ran into Jim at lunchtime today. Jim is my SpLD pupil from Corey's class last year, the child who couldn't write except in linguistic algorithms. He was standing in the rain outside the front of the school when I dashed out to have a smoke. He was half-drenched, plucking the leaves off a bush and looking very woebegone. I was woebegone myself – *seriously, this is fucking June and the rain hasn't quit since it began!* – but I asked Jim what was wrong. He told me to just go on. But I couldn't 'go on' because, as I said, I wanted a smoke and I couldn't light up in front of him. I pressed him to tell me what was up. Finally, he told me that some girl called Patricia had called him a dickhead and pushed him in technology class. He had then told her he was going to stick a pencil up her nose. On hearing this, the teacher had threatened Jim with lunch detention and refused to listen to his side of the story. In a strop, Jim had walked out. And here he was.

I told him I'd talk to the teacher. He said he didn't care.

'You're getting soaked, Jim,' I said. 'And I'm getting soaked.'

'Well then, just go on,' he says. 'I need you to go inside, Jim. I can't leave you standing here in the rain. You'll get pneumonia, and then you'll sicken and die and I'll never forgive myself. It'll haunt me the rest of my days, and I'll probably turn to the drink, and it'll kill me so you'll be responsible for killing the both of us.'

Not so much as a smile.

Didn't I tell you I was wasted?

'I'm not going,' he says.

'Look, Jim...' I says, looking at this poor, miserable, downtrodden child. I had to come up with something. I hadn't had a smoke since break-time. 'I'm on my lunch and I'm going for my lunch at my mom's house. I don't get to see her much. She's seventy-eight. Are you going to stop me seeing my old mom?' I laid it on a little thicker. 'She's all on her own, Jim.'

Jim considers this. He's a good kid and I knew this would work on him. He gives a tut. 'Oh, all right!' he says and swings his shoulders and walks back inside the school. I went round the corner, lit up, drew some fresh air into my asthmatic lungs and looked up into the rain, and thought about the hot sun in Magaluf, and lies, damned lies and statistics.

# 13 JUNE

*The supreme art of war is to subdue the enemy without fighting.*
SUN TZU

I covered a class about a month ago that I have since tried to banish from my memory. They were first years and the top class. Wee buns, easy money. I told them to get their books out and get on with some work. But they claimed they didn't have any work to do. I threatened them with my grammar book. Suddenly they did find work to do. As I say, wee buns.

Then I spy this little guy with this weird lopsided smile. He was a bag of bones, thin enough to blow away, and his every feature seemed to have been sharpened to a point. He looked like Mr Burns out of *The Simpsons*, or what Monty Burns would have looked like if he had ever been eleven and wasn't a cartoon character. Don't judge a book by its cover, right? Then again, first impressions count. I should have spotted trouble right from the off.

'What's your name?' I asked.

'Nathan,' he says, nice as pie.

I was nice as pie back. 'Nathan, get some work out, please.'

'Don't have any.'

I wasn't giving any more chances. I took a photocopied page from my grammar book and give him an exercise on speech marks. 'There, now you've got work to do.'

'Can I go to the bathroom?' he says.

'After you've finished the exercise.'

'But I have to wash my hands,' he says.

'After you finish the exercise.'

He went quiet. I went back to my desk. He stayed quiet for about thirty seconds. 'Why do I have to do this?' he says, meaning the exercise.

I had my own work to do. I had no time for this. I was brusque, no-nonsense: 'Because you've got no work of your own. That's the way this works. If you can't find work of your own then I provide you with work.'

He seemed to consider this, then repeated, 'Can I go to the bathroom?'

I gave him a look, my best you-don't-know-who-you're-fuckin-with-kid look. 'Get some work done first,' I said.

'But my hands are dirty.'

I took a breath. 'What's your problem, Nathan?'

'I've got dirty hands', says he.

This got a few laughs. The class were tuning in. I needed to hit this on the head. 'Get some work done and you can go wash your hands,' I said. 'Fair enough?'

'How much work?'

'Five questions,' I said. 'When you're on number five.'

He set to work. A few minutes later, his hand went up. 'Can I go to the bathroom now?' he said.

'Have you done five questions?' I asked.

'Four,' he said.

'I told you to do five and then you could go to the bathroom.'

'No, you said "when you're on number five" and I'm on number five.'

He was right. I had said that. At the same time, I hadn't. But now was the time to put an end to this, to smile, to laugh even, to defuse this whole thing and tell Nathan, 'OK, I did say that. Mea culpa. Go and wash your hands.' Instead, tired, fed up, my hackles rising at the end of a long day, after losing another goddamn free during which I can't get anything done because I'm having to deal with this crap, I raise my voice and repeat, 'Five questions!'

Predictably, Nathan raised his voice as well. 'You said "when you're on number five"!'

I didn't answer him.

'*I want to wash my hands!*' he yelled.

'*Out!*' I yelled.

I got him outside the class. 'I don't like you,' he kept repeating, louder and louder. I couldn't get a word in. A teacher came out of the class next door. I asked her who the hell this guy was, as in, shouldn't he be on news bulletins? She just rolled her eyes and said, 'That's Nathan,' as if that was all I needed to know. She seemed to know him well, though, and guided him into her room out of harm's way, leaving me feeling like a complete dickhead.

And rightly so.

One of the first things you're told as a teacher is never turn any exchange with a 'difficult' pupil into a zero-sum game. Problem is that a difficult pupil will often turn it into just such a game on the mildest of provocations. I had walked straight into a confrontation. I looked Nathan up on the SEN register. It made grim reading. He had the whole nine yards, basically, an alphabet soup of challenge. I couldn't have played this worse if I had tried. The 'question five' business… it made me want to shake my head and weep. Nathan was autistic, for God's sake!

That was a month ago. Now I'm covering Nathan and his class again. It's exam week and they have a Science exam after break. I say hello and get them all sitting down. Nathan is sitting directly in front of me. I tell the class to get on with their revision. They do what they're told… except for Nathan. The words of that celebrated twentieth-century thinker Björn Ulvaeus are on the tip of my tongue: 'Mamma mia, here we go again'.

Nathan doesn't get out any books.

I don't say anything.

He puts his head down on the table.

I don't say anything.

Then he lifts both his head and his hand.

Now I speak. 'Yes? Nathan, isn't it?' Oh, but I'm such a little tease.

'Can I go to the bathroom?'

Almost the exact same scenario. Which way do I play it? Last time, I made my permission conditional. This time, I make it unconditional. I'm not going to give him the slightest opportunity to say no to me.

'Go ahead,' I say.

He goes to the bathroom and returns three minutes later. He goes to his desk. He sits down. But he doesn't take out his books, which I had hoped might be the unspoken quid-pro-quo of the bathroom permission. Plan B is called for.

He's looking at me, waiting for me to say something. I'm the guy who blew his top last time. Nathan thinks there's some good-quality confrontation to be had here. But I pretend not to notice. I don't say a word. I'm not going to say a word. Five minutes go by, then ten. I'm getting on with my marking. Fifteen minutes go by. Finally, he puts up his hand.

'Yes, Nathan?' I'm so polite.

'What time is it?' he says. (In other words, 'Look at me, I haven't got any books out. What are you going to do about it, you bastard?')

'Twenty-five past nine, Nathan,' I tell him and go back to my work.

At half nine, I look up and Nathan is setting out his books. From then until eleven o'clock, he revises for his Science exam, not a peep out of him.

Mamma Mia!

# 20 JUNE

There was a time when reports were written by hand (I suppose there was a time when they were written with a quill). At that time, there was a box on the page for each subject and each subject teacher would write down Little Johnny's summer exam result, and a comment on this result, and whether or not it reflected Little Johnny's work during the preceding year, and what Little Johnny needed to continue doing or what he needed to put right. All in all, that was the basic gist of it.

That subject box wasn't huge, though. There was room for maybe two or three sentences. But that meant the sentences had to count. You had to say what you meant. Also, there was the physical act of putting pen to paper. That in itself made the comment more personal. Now, of course, reports are written up on the computer. Nothing wrong with that. Hey, I love computers. Some of my best friends are… I mean, have computers. But computers mean that those subject boxes aren't so small any more. In fact, they aren't small at all. They're fucking huge! You can write as much in those boxes as you like, and that's what teachers are encouraged to do: spaces need to be filled, boxes need to be ticked. Then again, longer is not necessarily better (I will resist the obvious bishop/chorus girl jokes). Recall that wisdom expressed at the end of a lengthy letter by the French mathematician and philosopher Blaise Pascal: 'I have made this longer than usual because I have not had time to make it shorter.'

Here's a report I filled in today:

Teacher's Comment: Lee has made progress across all three strands of English language this year – Reading, Writing and Talking and Listening. His work has been inconsistent at times but with focus I am confident he will continue to make progress. If I have an issue it is that his work can sometimes be hurried and homeworks have been missed. Vocabulary work – dictionary/thesaurus/ more reading – will aid his progress. Enjoy the break.

Communication Level: Lee fulfils the criteria for CCEA Communication Level 3. He can listen for specific information, understand and maintain a role. He can ask questions which will extend understanding. He can plan and sequence a talk so that it makes sense. He can vary expression and change tone effectively. He can use body language, pose, gesture, facial expression to convey a message. He can paraphrase a story. He can use a variety of reading strategies independently. He understands different forms and features of texts and can make deductions. He can ask and respond to questions for understanding.

He can talk about and plan his writing. He can use appropriate forms when writing and use basic punctuation and grammar. He can spell frequently used words correctly.

Never mind the quality, feel the width, eh?

As well as its length (and nonsense), the defining characteristic of this report is its positivity. That's the buzzword in education these days. Reports must be written in a spirit of positivity. Therefore the language is political in an Orwellian sense; words as obfuscation. In other words, truth goes out the window.

Re. Teacher's Comment, let me break that down for you:

'*Lee has made progress across all three strands of English language this year – Reading, Writing and Talking and Listening.*' This means Lee has made little or no progress. (I have five options in my comment bank – all teachers must use a store of comments otherwise, considering the length of reports, we'd be writing this verbiage until next summer. These options are '*satisfactory progress*', '*good progress*', '*very good progress*', '*excellent progress*' or simply '*progress*'. Choosing '*progress*' means the pupil is doing fuck all.)

'*His work has been inconsistent at times but with focus I am confident he will continue to make progress.*' As I said, doing fuck all, and will probably continue to do fuck all.

'*If I have an issue it is that his work can sometimes be hurried and homeworks have been missed.*' Work is a scrawl and couldn't give two shits about homework. And since it's called HOME work, is anybody at home going to get up off their arse and try to get him to do some? Does anyone at home give a damn?

'*Vocabulary work – dictionary/thesaurus/more reading – will aid his progress.*' Just saying, but it might be a good idea to open a book the odd time.

Regarding the sign-off line, I have five options in my comment bank:

'*Enjoy your well-deserved summer holiday.*' An excellent year's work.

'*Have a great summer holiday.*' A very good year's work.

'*Have a great summer.*' A good year's work.

'*Enjoy your summer.*' A satisfactory year's work.

Lastly, and this, of course, is Lee's:

'*Enjoy the break.*' I know *I* will, especially because I won't have to look at you for the next couple of months.

Besides the above, there are also those sins of omission. In my comment banks I have other lines such as '*Participates in all activities*', '*Always well-mannered and co-operative*', '*Works well with peers and adults*' and '*A pleasure to teach*'. These aren't present in Lee's report. Why not? Well, because he doesn't participate in all activities, and he isn't well-mannered and co-operative, and he doesn't work well with peers and adults, and he definitely isn't a pleasure to teach; rather, he's a pain in the ass to teach and he's the reason so many teachers apply for early redundancy. But to write all that would be extremely negative. In fact, you can't get much more negative. So I just leave all that out. Don't want to be giving anybody a complex.

Then we move on to the Communication Levels. Or let's not, says you. Aren't they a mouthful? Honestly, did you ever read such shit in your life? O what made fatuous sunbeams toil to break earth's sleep at all? But, again, it's 'he can... he can... he can...' Positive, positive, positive.

The upshot is that a pupil who is acting the complete bollix a lot of the time, and who is often ill-mannered and rude, and who doesn't do his homework, and who can't be trusted to behave like a human being in close proximity to other human beings, is made to seem... well, like he's doing OK. Not brilliant, but OK. At least he hasn't knifed anybody or set fire to the school or taken a dump on a teacher's desk, right? And with just a little more concentration, some focus, a few pats on the back or words in his shell-like, he'll be right as rain and skipping out of those school gates in a few years' time with a bunch of qualifications to his name, happy as a pig in shite, ready to become a model citizen.

A complete and utter untruth but, hey, nobody's feelings are getting hurt, and maybe with this kind of positivity – this kind of 'can do' rather than 'can't do' spirit – instead of Lee concluding that he's pulled the wool over everybody's eyes and why not try the same shit again (especially when he got rewarded with a Boneless Banquet Fun Bucket at KFC for getting such a good report), maybe he will suddenly undergo a Damascene conversion.

Yeah, right!

By the way, I slept in this morning. First time all year. Knocked off the snooze button by mistake. Anyway, I was twenty minutes late. Another teacher was covering my first class so I raced down to her room and apologised and went to grab my class. But a mighty groan went up. They were watching *Friends*. Emphasising the greater educational opportunities available in my room, I gathered them up, marched them to my classroom and grabbed the first thing to hand off the shelf, because I was now behind with my reports and I needed to get a shift on. But that first thing to hand happened to be *Men in Black* and five minutes later no one – *and I mean no one!* – was watching it.

Piece o' shit!

# 25 JUNE

We got our training on Differentiation today.

Remember that?

To give the senior management team their due, it was more than a perfunctory hour's worth of platitudes, as I suggested it might be. No, it was a full day's worth of them. The guy who was conducting the training opened it by playing a video of a teacher conducting a class on poetry where the teacher didn't explain the poem she wanted the class to study. Not only that, she didn't even read it out. Instead, she divided the class into groups and handed out random lines from the poem for the pupils to assemble in some kind of order. They were then to justify their arrangement of the lines. We got about three minutes of this video but the idea was clear enough: this was about the pupils and not the teacher. Instead of the teacher explaining the poem to the pupils, the pupils were to take charge.

I could see holes in this, but I was as judicious as the editing and kept my mouth shut.

From the snippets of lines, I worked out the poem and

the poet. However, as with the theme of the training, this knowledge was surplus to requirements: the training guy didn't ask about either. Yes, this was different – empty your mind, leave your book-learning at the door. The rest of the session consisted of various strategies and examples of classroom practice where the guy or gal at the front of the room, i.e. the teacher, was 'facilitating learning' rather than 'dispensing knowledge'.

Hmm.

My personal favourite was one written up by a sub teacher. The class were studying *Romeo and Juliet* but the sub hadn't read it. In fact, not only had he not read it but he didn't know the story. I ask myself: should people like this really be allowed into schools? Anyhow, he didn't let his ignorance hold him back. Rather, he flaunted it and just started shooting off random questions – Who was Romeo? Who was Juliet? What was their problem? How did they try to solve their problem? – and by the end of twenty minutes, instead of the kids asking him where he got his lobotomy, he had a really good idea of the play and the pupils were in animated discussion about theme, imagery and characterisation. The sub finished by saying it was the best lesson he had 'taught' all year.

There you go; it's just like magic, and ignorance isn't just bliss, it is to be actively encouraged.

I mean, is this where we are?

*Is this where we fucking are?*

I was sitting beside an RE teacher. She burst out laughing

at one point. I could have done with a laugh so I read what she was reading. It was a lesson where pupils were to use Play-Doh to create a physical representation of the Holy Spirit. I laughed too.

Who are these great kids who aren't firing Play-Doh at one another or sculpting huge penises out of it?

Where do these people teach?

There was another lesson – don't ask me what kind of lesson, or the details; it was late on and I was concentrating on my breathing in case I flatlined – where the idea was that students were divided into groups and they were to communicate whatever conclusions they had reached in their group by writing them on a page, making a paper aeroplane out of said page, and then throwing this to a group on the other side of the room.

*I'm not fucking joking!*

Such tremendous fun!

Of differentiation, which is what this training was supposed to be about, I don't think I heard the word mentioned after the initial introduction. Applied to the last lesson, maybe differentiation is the smart one in the group making the paper aeroplane then handing it to the stupid one to throw it.

I don't know.

Beats me.

# 28 JUNE

Last day.

Time to quote Alice Cooper. Not 'School's out for the summer', though. You must know me better than that by now. I would never be so clichéd. No, I'm thinking of another of Alice's apposite reflections: 'It doesn't matter how many drugs I take, I'm not fulfilled.'

School finished at midday. There was a get-together in the staffroom – sandwiches and scones. I wished my colleagues a good summer then left. A lot of the staff were going for a meal and a few drinks. I don't do that any more. Too many times, I had too many drinks and said something I shouldn't and fretted about it for weeks over the holidays.

So I leave and pop into my mom's, into that quiet house where the horse racing is no longer blaring and my da isn't calling some jockey a bastard. That silence still unnerves me. It will always unnerve me, I suppose. Max Porter titled his poem-story about bereavement *Grief is the Thing with Feathers*. In our house, it's 'Grief is the thing with an e-cigarette'. That's my mom, sucking on an e-cig since my father died, having given up the fags. She keeps telling me to quit, especially now with my asthma. Maybe I will quit.

What about the fags, says you.

I chat to Mom about this and that – and no matter what this or that is, she finds some way to reference my father – and then I go home. I've got painting to do. My summer project. Not oils or watercolours, though; no, I'm painting the house. What's that line in *The Producers*? 'Hitler, there was a painter. He could paint an entire apartment in one afternoon – two coats!'

Yeah, me and Adolf. I remember when 9H were studying *The Boy in the Striped Pyjamas* before Christmas and I told them about Hitler's original family name, Schicklgruber. That tickled them. We discussed whether a man with a funny name like Schicklgruber would have been taken quite as seriously as a man called Hitler. Would the Holocaust or the Second World War have happened if Adolf Hitler had been called Adolf Schicklgruber? What's in a name, eh? We pondered Juliet's contention, 'A rose by any other name would smell as sweet.' In very basic terms, without referencing Barthes, Derrida or Foucault – oh, who's a clever boy? – I explained the post-structuralist idea of the signified and the signifier, that words are just a random assembly of sounds to which we give meaning i.e. words as a totally human construct. From that we moved on to music: that music was the purest form of communication, that those seven basic notes had been recognisable in any language since the beginning of time. Was music, then, a human construct? After that, we took a leap. Music made us feel good, right? Since we had established that music was the purest form of communication, did it make us feel good because it spoke to something deep within ourselves of which we were not even aware? Something, perhaps, which might not be of human origin? What if that thing of which we were not aware was our soul? What if music made us feel good because when we sang or played an instrument we were reaching towards the divine? What if music was a prayer?

Thinking about it, though, another way to do that lesson would have been to divide the class into groups and have each group decide on the most important thing they knew about Hitler. Once they had decided on their 'fact', they could have written it out on a piece of paper with the coloured marker provided and then made a paper aeroplane out of it…

Ha!

I wrote my resignation letter. That talk on differentiation – as much as it was on differentiation – made up my mind. But the Principal wasn't in this morning. She was at a conference in Belfast. She'll be in school the first week of the holidays, doing some administration.

I'll present it to her then.

I hope these entries demonstrate the reality of this job and how it is becoming more and more difficult. Teachers are being squeezed. The pips are squeaking. We are not adequately resourced or trained or paid. Those in positions of power have to decide whether they want to invest in the future or not. That's the bottom line. And investing in the future doesn't mean more inspections or more testing. It doesn't mean more analysis of output; it means more attention to input.

I got talking to that senior manager I mentioned before, the one who was retiring. I wished him luck. He repeated all his reasons for leaving and then talked about the number of SEN pupils he was teaching. The numbers seemed to be just going up and up... and he had no idea how to teach them. Simply no idea. There they were, on his rolls, and he was scratching his head as to what to do with them. He said that this wasn't right – it was unfair to these kids and their parents and it was unfair to him since it left him feeling utterly useless.

I recognise that feeling, and reading back through these entries I recognise other things too. I recognise a frustration and, more than that, an anger, and even more than that... a terrible cynicism. A cynic may be a failed romantic, as Oscar Wilde claimed, but nevertheless, that's still a cynic. And that's the bottom line for me. I do not like the person I have become in this job – this snarling, wolfish man.

I have a chart on one of my walls (close to the glory hole). It's called 'Developing a Growth Mindset'. It reads:

| INSTEAD OF | TRY THINKING |
| --- | --- |
| I'm no good at this | What am I missing? |
| I give up | I'll use a different strategy |
| It's good enough | Is this really my best work? |

| I can't make this any better | I can always improve |
| This is too hard | This may take some time |
| I made a mistake | Mistakes help me to learn |
| I just can't do this | I am going to train my brain |
| I'll never be that smart | I will learn how to do this |
| Plan A didn't work | There's always Plan B |
| My friend can do it | I will learn from them |

Almost every class, I ask the kids to make the leap from the first column to the second.

But as things stand, after twenty-five years in this job – to paraphrase Marilyn Monroe: 'Quarter of a century – makes a boy think' – I myself can no longer make that leap.

Yes, my mind's made up.

Yes, it is...